TERRY LOVELL

PICTURES OF REALITY
Aesthetics, Politics, Pleasure

1980
BFI Publishing

THE AUTHOR

Terry Lovell is a Lecturer in Sociology at the University of Warwick, where she teaches a course on the Sociology of Knowledge and Literature. She has written for *Screen* and the *European Journal of Sociology*, and has also contributed to *Sociology of Literature* (Diana Laurenson, ed., Sociological Review Monograph, 1978) and *Sociology of Mass Communications* (Denis McQuail, ed., Penguin 1972).

Published by the British Film Institute
127 Charing Cross Road
London WC2H OEA

Cover design: Mario Lippa

Copyright © British Film Institute 1980

ISBN 0 85170 102 7 (hardcover)
ISBN 0 85170 103 5 (paperback)

Printed by Tonbridge Printers Limited, Tonbridge, Kent.

Contents

FOR ALAN

Acknowledgments

This work is an expansion and development of a paper which was first written in 1978, and of which a revised version appears in S. Clarke *et al.*, *One Dimensional Marxism* (1980). Due to their common origin, there is a certain amount of overlap between the two papers, but the idea of writing an expanded work on these issues arose out of discussions of the original paper. I should like to thank the members of the Film Study Group at Berkeley during Spring 1978, the Conference of Socialist Economists, Summer 1978, and the Birmingham and Coventry Feminist Research Workshop, with whom these discussions took place. My thanks are also due to Roy Enfield, Peter Fairbrother, Phil Fryer and Alan Lovell for their detailed comments on earlier drafts, with the usual disclaimer of responsibility on their part for remaining errors and inadequacies. I would also like to thank Angela Martin and Geoffrey Nowell-Smith for their valuable editorial work.

Introduction

This work comes from a long-standing interest in the arts and mass culture as social phenomena and in the search for some way of placing these phenomena within social structures and relations. The sociological tradition, even at its most totalising theoretical heights, has failed to confront this task. The reasons for this failure are complex and puzzling. Art is found in all known societies. It is ubiquitous as religion and, on the face of it, no less important as a social phenomenon. Yet in the sociological tradition the neglect of the one is only matched by the obsession with the other. Sociologists have never exhibited the same wariness of and willingness to defer to the expertise of specialist disciplines associated with religion as they have the arts. On the whole they have gladly accepted an intellectual division of labour which reserves 'great art' for critics, and leaves 'mass art' to the sociologist. Yet religion has been treated within classical sociology as almost *the* sociological phenomenon *par excellence,* while art has been utterly marginalised. It is generally accepted that art *is* a social phenomenon and, as such, that sociological concepts may have some purchase upon it. But it has never been given a central place in sociological theory, even among those sociologists who highlight in their theories what they term 'expressive symbol systems'. There is of course a sizable body of writings on the history of art which attempts to place art in its socio-historical context, and this is frequently the best we have, so far as a sociology of art is concerned. But this cannot absolve sociology from the task of developing an approach to art as an integral part of the complex of social relations and institutions which it studies, as important as that occupied by work, the family, religion, etc.

Of the three major branches of classical sociology, only marxism has given rise to any substantial body of writings on art. Weber wrote a slim monograph on music which no-one reads. Otherwise he had no professional interest in the arts. While Durkheim's work on symbolic forms, from primitive classifications to religions, has interesting possibilities, he wrote nothing directly upon art. Some of the major contributors to German neo-Kantian sociology, such as Simmel and Scheler, were, it is true, concerned with aesthetics to a greater extent than Weber. But Simmel is remembered in the history of sociology for his work on small groups and not for his aesthetics. This strand of neo-Kantian aesthetic sociology has not been incorporated in the work of its heirs. Rather it has joined the stream of marxist sociology of art, where these two intellectual traditions *(neo-Kantian sociology and Hegelian marxism) converge in the work of Georg Lukács. This is one of the reasons why Lukács is such a seminal figure for the sociology of art.

Marxist cultural studies has been given a tremendous boost in the past decade by the success of Althusserian marxism in colonising this area. Yet the direction in which Althusserianism, supported by Lacanian psychoanalysis and by semiology, has taken cultural studies is disturbing in relation to the marxist promise of a *sociology* of the arts. The most striking characteristic of this work is rather its insistence on the distance which separates the 'relatively autonomous' practices of cultural production from the remaining 'practices' which together constitute the social formation. Indeed 'sociology' has almost become a term of abuse in this work. Thus while much of the work that has come out of Althusserian cultural studies is impressive, it has made its gains at the expense of the project of a marxist sociology, the project of placing art within the structure of social relations.

While this move away from social determinations and effects differentiates Althusserian cultural studies from its marxist predecessors, it shares with them certain common features. Marxists who wished to theorise the relationship between art and society have always marked off 'high art' from mere ideology. Althusser, like Lukács before him, reserves for 'great art' a privileged place, distinct from but akin to knowledge. For Lukács, the 'great artist' was a 'partisan for the truth' and, by that token, for the proletarian revolution and socialism, whatever his/her overt politics. Art was seen by Lukács as a special kind of knowledge, in some ways superior to that generated by science. For Althusser, art is not knowledge, but maintains a close relationship to it:

> Art (I mean authentic art, not works of an average or mediocre level) does not give us a *knowledge* in the *strict sense,* it does not replace knowledge (in the modern sense: scientific knowledge), but what it gives us does nevertheless maintain a certain *specific relationship* with knowledge . . . I believe that the peculiarity of art is 'to make us see', 'make us perceive', 'make us feel', something which *alludes* to reality. (Althusser, 1977b, p204)

While these circumlocutions are distinctly unclear as to the exact nature of this 'specific relationship' which art maintains with knowledge, they do establish that for Althusser 'authentic art' has more in common with scientific knowledge than it has with 'art of an average or mediocre level'. That, presumably, can be discussed entirely within the category of ideology. In general, within marxist theories of art, mass art, where it has been discussed at all, has been dismissed as the artistically worthless product and instrument of bourgeois ideology. The single exception to this blanket dismissal is found in the marxism of Brecht and Benjamin, who were deeply interested in popular forms and in the technological developments of the mass media. Yet Brechtianism in contemporary film criticism and practice has, with few exceptions, been appropriated for the avant-garde rather than the commercial cinema. Brecht himself found it impossible to work within Hollywood.

This bifurcation between 'great art' and 'mass art' can be seen most strongly in the 'critical theory' of the Frankfurt School, one of the few schools of marxism to have devoted much attention to the analyisis of mass art. Horkheimer, Adorno and Marcuse centred their analysis around the commodity form of mass culture under monopoly capitalism. It was the penetration of capital which transformed art into a commodity and thereby robbed it of its critical, negating role in relation to capitalist society. As a commodity, mass art was tied to the ideological purposes of capitalism. Its audience was one of passive consumers, spoon-fed with 'entertainment' which made no demands upon them. Consumption and leisure mirrored the alienated world of work under capitalist commodity production. Both equally denied 'man's species being'.

Despite the limitations of this analysis, the current neglect of the Frankfurt School within contemporary cultural studies is unfortunate. It neglects the one strand of marxism which at least raised the question of the effects of the particular historical conditions of the production and consumption of works of art, and some interesting contemporary work in Germany on the consumption and production of art draws upon this tradition, while departing from it in other respects.* But the Frankfurt School was so unremittingly hostile to mass culture and entertainment that its engagement with it was bound to remain superficial, compared to its interest in high bourgeois culture. A more substantial sociology of mass art could only come from a more positive engagement with it — from the felt experience of its power to move, to create enjoyment.

In England, this kind of engagement came from the left, out of 'left Leavisism'. Part of its drive certainly came from the pedagogic urge to arm people against the seductions of mass culture, as can be seen in Denys Thompson's *Discrimination and Popular Culture*. But equally strong was the impulse to defend mass culture: to discriminate what was valuable, to celebrate what was authentic and enjoyable. This double intention can be seen at its best in Hall and Whannel's *Popular Arts*. In France, the same kind of positive engagement went into *Cahiers du Cinéma*'s 'auteur' theory. By contrast with left Leavisism, auteur theory was a-political or even reactionary. But in both cases the work was

*See E. Knodler-Bunte, 'The Proletarian Public Sphere and Political Organisation', *New German Critique*, No. 4, 1975.

rooted in the felt influence of American popular culture — cinema, but also music, detective fiction and other forms. In France there was *Cahiers* and, with the New Wave, the impact of its ideas upon film-making. The English thrust became institutionalised with the setting up of the Centre for Contemporary Cultural Studies in Birmingham in 1964. Both English and French currents returned finally to marxism. The CCCS, under Stuart Hall, became increasingly involved with Althusserian marxism in the seventies, while the post–1968 *Cahiers* has taken the same turn.

In the case of *Cahiers* this rather belated politicisation has lead to a certain guilty heart-searching over the many hours spent in watching and relishing American movies, now seen as products of American cultural imperialism. In a famous editorial* *Cahiers* developed a classification for a variety of films in terms of their differential relationship to bourgeois ideology. They accepted that film-making inevitably occupied the terrain of 'ideological practice', unlike their rivals, *Cinéthique,* who held that it might be transformed into 'theoretical practice'. But they might hope nevertheless, taking their cue from Althusser's own distancing of 'authentic art' from ideology, to rescue their most favoured directors. They argued that while the bulk of commercial films simply gave clear passage to bourgeois ideology, others succeeded in blocking or deflecting it, or in turning ideology in upon itself so that its own processes became visible. The films hailed as achieving this deflection were usually the same films which had previously been acclaimed as the work of 'auteurs'. The net effect was in both cases the same — to reproduce within 'mass art' the division which had earlier been placed between 'great art' and 'mass art' within the marxist tradition. There was, however, a difference of emphasis between auteur theory and *Cahiers'* new critique of ideology. Auteur theory pushed further and further into the reaches of what had been dismissed as commercial rubbish, as more and more directors were hailed as auteurs. The thrust of Althusserianism works on the whole in the opposite direction, towards a disengagement from commercial cinema and an increasing interest in a 'high culture' avant-garde.

This tendency is not, it is true, characteristic of the work of the CCCS, which has remained through all its theoretical vicissitudes committed to the study of popular culture. And it is interesting that its borrowings from Althusser have been largely confined to those aspects of his theory which are closest to the work of Gramsci. Gramsci's cultural theory allows for a different kind of engagement with popular culture to that sanctioned by the other, more original part of Althusser's theory of ideology, the theory of 'ideology in general'. The work of the various (and disparate) writers associated with *Screen* in this country has drawn

*Jean-Louis Comolli and Jean Narboni, 'Cinema/Ideology/Criticism', translated in *Screen,* v12, n1, Spring 1971; see also *Screen,* v12, n2 and v13, n1, for the continuing debate between *Cahiers* and *Cinéthique* (also available in *Screen Reader* 1, SEFT, London 1977.

much more heavily than the CCCS on this second part of Althusser's theory and upon the Lacanian theory of the subject which informs it. It is in this work centred around *Screen* that the relative disengagement from popular culture and the shift to the avant-garde can be seen most clearly.

Thus what is new in Althusserian marxism takes cultural studies away from an engagement with popular art, except in the negative form of ideological critique. This latter activity paradoxically brings us back close to the defensive positions of *Discrimination and Popular Culture*. It also moves away from the project of developing a sociology of art which places art in relation to social structures and relations. The Althusserian intervention has also created certain very real problems for students which have the effect of reinforcing these tendencies. They are under pressure from their teachers to come to terms with three very different and demanding intellectual traditions as a condition for doing cultural studies. To understand semiology, the student must dip into modern linguistic theory; to understand Lacan, s/he must go back to Freud, the post-freudians, and subsequent debates in psychoanalysis; to understand Althusser, a return to Marx and the long history of marxism is necessary, to say nothing of the need to know something of the history of capitalism. And all this in addition to reading the more specialised literature on cultural production itself — on film, television, etc. But many students of marxist cultural studies have come to their marxism through their interest in film and the media, rather than through political experience or an interest in history. Naturally their relationship to this formidable set of demands upon their time and intellect is coloured by this fact. In the circumstances it is hardly surprising that the losers in this competition for students' time and attention are those texts which are perceived as being furthest removed from the 'specificity' of cultural production. The particular stress of Althusserian marxism upon the specificity of cultural production and the relative autonomy of 'ideological practice' determines that the loser will be marxist historiography and the writings of Marx himself — all those texts which generate knowledge of the societal context of cultural production. As one commentator on Althusserianism recently put it: 'Reading *For Marx* becomes a substitute for reading Marx, and reading *Reading Capital* for reading *Capital*.' (Clarke, 1980, p11). Althusser's theory of semiautonomous practices not only licenses but enjoins specialisation in the understanding of particular practices in their specificity *before* they can be studied in their articulation with the remaining practices of the social formation. Inevitably the second task is postponed to a last instance which never comes.

There can be no doubt that this insistence upon the specificity of cultural production has been a welcome antidote to an all too prevalent sociological reductionism. But it merely reproduces the obverse of that reductionism in refusing the whole project of a sociology of art. Fear of sociological reductionism has closed certain avenues prematurely. Yet Althusser's interpretation of Marx is a very particular one, radically different from others which inform much marxist historiography. An exclusive exposure to Althusserian marxism cuts students off from the mainstream of marxist thought and work, which centres as it must upon history. Althusserianism has been successful in pre-empting the field of marxist cultural studies, in establishing itself in the universities, and in identifying itself as such with marxist theory. Alternative approaches to cultural studies from non-Althusserian marxism are passed over. In particular, approaches which begin from the 'social totality' (whether that 'totality' is seen as an 'expressive' or a 'structural' one) are rejected out of hand on the basis of a few arguments against 'marxist humanism'. Of course the danger of 'totalising marxism' of either variety is that of reductionism. But this is a danger inherent in the whole project of developing a sociology of art. It is certainly avoided by insisting upon the autonomy of art, and studying it as an independent practice. But this solution is a defeat, not only for sociology of art but for marxist cultural studies, whose own 'specificity' is precisely the attempt to interrelate the apparently disparate practices of the social formation.

The various attempts to place art within its societal context have frequently been associated with an aesthetics of realism and have concentrated upon those realist works which are most obviously 'about' society and social relations. Certainly any sociology of art must confront first and foremost the question of the relationships which exist between art and social reality, relationships both at the level of meaning and of cause/effect. This is the first reason why realism is a recurrent topic in marxist cultural studies. To this may be added the fact that the major thrust of Althusserian marxist cultural studies has been centred around a critique of realist theory and practice in art. There is no concept in the history of aesthetics which has generated more confusions, and no area, from the point of view of developing a sociology of art, where greater clarity is required. To investigate realism in art is immediately to enter into philosophical territory — into questions of ontology and epistemology: of what exists in the world, and how that world can be known.

Althusserian cultural studies stakes its claim to superiority over left Leavisism and auteur theory in its claim to have inaugurated a science. I want to argue that this claim has been made on the basis of a misrecognition both of the nature of science and of marxist epistemology. This has been a direct consequence of the vacating of marxist cultural studies from the ground mapped out by the project of sociology of art, a project intrinsic to marxism. It has also led to the loss of some of the ground gained by each of these earlier interventions in the study of mass culture. In order to assess the scientistic claims of Althusser it will be necessary to ask the reader to engage with yet another body of literature, that of philosophy of science. This is unavoidable if Althusserian marxism, in its impact upon cultural studies, is to be assessed in its own chosen terms, and if the relationship between social reality and cultural production is to be investigated. Althusser himself locates cultural production in relation to 'ideological practice', and the concept of ideology has remained as a result one of the chief organising concepts of marxist cultural studies. Therefore it will be necessary to raise the question of the nature and status of the concept of ideology, and the companion question, never far distant, of science. To do this it is necessary to move beyond Althusser's own writings to a consideration of the literature, marxist and non-marxist, where these questions have been posed and answered.

This work has two aims. The first is to assess Althusserian marxism in its impact upon cultural studies by and through a consideration of the epistemological issues which Althusser addresses in his writings, and in so doing to direct attention to a broader range of marxist and non-marxist texts than are usually cited by Althusserians on these questions. Secondly, to return to marxist categories in an attempt to adumbrate a marxist theory of mass culture (i.e. a theroretical investigation of the meaningful and causal relationships between art, mass culture and society) and to identify actual and possible marxist approaches which might prove useful in this task.

The first chapter develops the argument that marxism has a realist theory of knowledge and society. To establish this thesis fully would take all the space available and more. All that can be done here is to introduce the reader to the debates within which this thesis has been established, and to draw out some of its implications for marxism and cultural studies. In a sense this is the most important part of the work, for the whole of the remainder of the text depends upon this thesis being accepted. Some of the issues raised may be unfamiliar to many readers, but I hope that they will bear with me through these initial abstractions, and will see the relevance that they have for cultural studies. For the kind of cultural studies which is developed depends upon the explicit or implicit positions adopted on these epistemological questions. Althusser, to his credit, is consistently explicit. The same cannot always be said of his followers.

The second chapter develops a critique of Althusser and the post-Althusserians which centres on their theory of science and ideology, in relation to the defence of epistemological realism in the first chapter. The third chapter spells out some of the implications of the first two for the development of a concept and theory of ideology and explores the ideological consequences of the penetration of capital into cultural production. The fourth and fifth chapters look at marxist theories of art in the light of marxism's realist epistemology and examine the relationship between this epistemological realism and 'realism' in art. Lukács's attempt to develop a marxist realist aesthetics is examined, and also three different types of critique of realism.

The first of these critiques is mounted from within the major premiss of realism itself, namely the proposition that it is the task of art 'to show things as they really are'. This critique is associated with the work of Brecht, and is directed against the conventions of realism. The second is mounted from a diametrically opposed epistemological position, that of conventionalism, and it challenges not only the conventions of realism but its goal. It argues that since art cannot 'show things as they really are', realist art which pretends to do this identifies itself as producing not a mirror to reality but the illusion of the real. This critique is associated with conventionalist marxist cultural studies. The third accepts the epistemological realism shared by Marx, Lukács and Brecht, accepts also much of Brecht's critique of Lukács, as well as some aspects of the conventionalist critique, while rejecting its conventionalist base. It challenges the assumption that the realist goal of 'showing things as they really are' follows from marxist epistemological realism and material-ism. It draws attention to other aspects of art besides its knowledge function — to questions of pleasure, questions of politics.

Marxism is a Realism

In this chapter I want to establish the proposition that marxism is a realism. It posits a social world which consists in a complex structure of social relations which are produced by the dominant mode of production and reproduction of material life. The social world is emphatically not, for Marx, the product of either theoretical work, or of the consciousness of individuals or groups. It cannot be *known* without the work of theory construction, and that work of theory construction and the consciousness that individuals and groups have of the social world is itself part of that world.

It is necessary to establish these fundamental propositions about marxism in order to assess recent developments in marxist cultural studies, because of the extent to which these developments rest upon a qualification or even refusal of the philosophy of realism. To establish these propositions in even the most cursory form it is necessary to engage with some of the debates which have occupied the literature of philosophy of science over a considerable period of time. These debates tend not to be well known among students of cultural studies. This creates a double problem. For the issues are complex and require more than the few pages available here for full exposure. Anyone who knows of these debates only through the brief introduction advanced here will probably remain perplexed. Therefore this chapter serves only to establish a prima facie case that marxism is a realism, and to explore some of the consequences which follow for marxist theories of cultural production. In particular, the development of such theories on the basis of a non-realist account of language and culture becomes immediately problematic. This does not matter, of course, for non-marxists, or for marxists who believe that marxism can be reinterpreted as a form of conventionalism which is commensurable with these conventionalist theories of language. But the problematic nature of marxist convention-alism in cultural studies must be faced, on peril of intellectual confusion of the first order, by those who become convinced that what is most valuable in the marxist theory of society and history depends upon a philosophy which is irreconcilable with conventionalist theories of cultural production.

In order to convince readers who have become familiar with precisely such conventionalist marxism through marxist cultural studies, that marxism is a realism, it will be necessary for them to read beyond these pages. One of the tasks of this chapter is to introduce the sources where this proposition is more fully established than it can be here, and to convince readers on the basis of the prima facie case that it will prove worthwhile or even necessary to pursue this matter further.

Realism is both a theory of knowledge and an ontology (an account of what exists and is real in the world). Two recent important contributions to the philosophy of social science (Benton, 1977; Keat and Urry, 1975) concur in identifying three major types of theory of knowledge, of which realism is one. These theories might perhaps more properly be described as 'limit positions' around which theories of knowledge cluster. The first which they identify is positivism,* although the more generic term might be empiricism. Positivism is, they argue, logically incoherent. It cannot provide an account of the processes of knowledge production in which scientists are actually engaged in their day-to-day activities, nor of the history of science. The second position is known as conventionalism, and is the source of a devastating critique of positivism and empiricism. But conventionalism is undermined by its inability to avoid relativism. The third position, realism, shares with positivism and empiricism the belief in the existence of an independent reality and thus avoids relativism. Yet it also claims to be able to avoid the conventionalist critique which cripples positivism and empiricism.

The context of the development of modern epistemological realism is what has been termed the 'Copernican Revolution' in the philosophy of science. The prehistory of this revolution goes back to the early rationalist challenge to empiricism, as we shall see.

I. EMPIRICISM

i. Empiricism and 'the Real'

Empiricism embraces a wide variety of philosophical theories of knowledge. All theories of knowledge have ontological implications — implications about what the world is like and what things exist in it. Empiricist ontology posits a real world which is independent of consciousness and theory, and which is accessible through sense-experience. To be a candidate for (empirical) reality, something must be capable of generating actual or possible experiences. But by making sense-experience the sole criterion of the real empiricism achieves a

*There is an enormous literature on positivism and its history. Positivism consists basically in the belief that 'positive knowledge' can only be obtained by the methods used by the natural sciences, and what cannot be known through those methods is unknowable. It is also committed to an empiricist account of scientific method, the doctrine that the source and foundation of knowledge is in the experience of objects of the external world, through the senses. The term positivism was coined by Auguste Comte, who developed the first systematic positivist sociology.

fusion between what *is* and what can be *known*. Ontology is reduced to epistemology; what is to what can be known. As Roy Bhaskar remarks, in characterising the empiricist position:

> . . . only perception gives knowledge of things . . . hence knowledge must be of what is given in perception. Thus on the one hand only items directly given in sense-experience may be said to be known to exist; and on the other, the world may now . . . be regarded as constituted by facts which are given as the real objects of experience . . . (Bhaskar, 1975, p33)*

Empiricism is premised on the existence of a knowing subject, source of the sense data which validates knowledge. This knowing subject and its experience are taken as given and unproblematic by empiricism, or, where it is problematised, empiricism begins to be undermined.

ii. Empiricism, Knowledge Production and the Knowing Subject

In its simplest form, empiricism sees the process of knowledge production as a matter of careful, objective recording of empirical regularities. These regularities are established by induction (reasoning from particular to general) on the basis of the observation of the behaviour of particular things under experimentally controlled conditions. Rigorous controls in the production of empirical data are necessary because of the danger of slipping into subjectivist error. For the particular individual subjects whose sense experience provides the data may err. They may lapse in their attention, may suffer from delusions, or may distort their experiences in the direction of what they hope or expect to find. Therefore empiricism insists that the sense data of science must be repeatable, regular, and in principle open to any investigator.

For simple empiricism, then, knowledge is determined by nature or reality, and is mediated by the experiences of the knowing subject. From its inception empiricism has been troubled by the subjective side of this process, the input of the knowing subject. Empiricists such as Locke and Bacon were concerned to find ways of eliminating subjective error, so that objective reality could be given untrammelled passage through the mediations of sense-experience. The earliest critics of empiricism seized upon this difficuly in a more positive manner, and proclaimed an active and necessary part for the mind in the construction of knowledge. The

---

*The concept of 'facts' is ambiguous as between 'states of affairs in the world' and elementary propositions about the world. It is this shift of meaning which permits the illusion that 'facts' belong simultaneously to two orders, the order of being, and the order of concepts. The problem of relating these two orders appears to be solved if there is a substratum of 'facts' which belongs to both.

It seems best to recognise the relationship between 'facts' and theories/conceptual schema by placing them firmly within the order of concepts rather than things. 'Facts' always take the form of propositions. But they *refer* to states of affairs in the world.

mind was not to be viewed negatively as an unfortunate source of potential error, the necessary but flawed instrument through which the real world was opened to knowledge, but as central to the whole process of knowledge production. For the rationalist, knowledge was not a reflection in consciousness of the real world, but something actively constructed through the use of mental constructs — concepts, theories, methodological rules, etc. These mental constructs which are the working tools of knowledge production are not given with the data of experience which they are used to understand. Classical idealism saw these mental constructs as the free creations of the human mind, and it could continue to claim objective status for knowledge only if these free creations could be shown to have some objective base. Kant located their objectivity in the universal and necessary characteristics of knowledge — what he termed the 'synthetic *a prioris*' which he held to be conditions of any possible knowledge. He included such general organising concepts as that of space, time and causality. Perhaps the most notorious attempt to escape relativism and subjectivism was that of Bishop Berkeley, who claimed that the world's objectivity was guaranteed by God. It had objective existence only as an idea in the mind of God. But inevitably a fully fledged relativism and subjectivism was placed upon the agenda in the philosophy of knowledge. It was only a matter of time before someone took the bull by the horns and celebrated a relativism which could not be avoided.

Subjectivism, the first precursor of conventionalism, is a celebration of human freedom and creativity. Conventionalism departs only in locating that freedom not in each individual, but in the collectivity, the knowledge community. The development of conceptual frames of reference, theories and methods is held by conventionalism to depend upon shared conventions established within the scientific community, or within language itself.

iii. Empiricism and the Language of Theory

The rationalist insistence upon the critical importance of concepts, theories and methodological rules in knowledge production was the source of the first challenge to empiricism. It forced recognition that knowledge was not something given with and in the reality it knew, but a human construct, the result of certain kinds of mental activity. The problem of accounting for the generation and role of theory in knowledge production was one which all succeeding and more sophisticated empiricisms have had to confront. The most obvious way to try to resolve this problem was by treating theoretical terms as coded summaries of empirical knowledge. All references to theoretical entities were held to be shorthand summaries of empirical data. Another solution was to treat them as convenient or necessary fictions, useful in generating empirical knowledge, but not in themselves entailing any reality-claim. The theoretical furniture of 'forces', 'atoms', etc. were to be treated as heuristic fictions unless and until some corresponding empirical referent could be found. For instance, a simple apparatus known as the 'Wilson cloud-chamber' is used to track the emissions from radioactive substances and other small elementary particles. The ability to generate these empirical phenomena would justify elevating the status of such elementary particles from convenient fictions, to existence in reality. This interpretation of theories and theoretical terms was given some support by the coexistence of two incompatible theories of light in nineteenth-century physics. The wave and the particle models of light equally accounted for the known facts, a given set of empirical phenomena. They were used as convenience dictated according to the particular needs of the work in hand. Obviously reality claims could not be sustained for both models, as they were incompatible. Their continued use side by side could only be justified if it were held that neither made existence claims, and that such models were merely convenient heuristic tools.

iv. Empiricism, the Language of Observation and Empirical Testing

Both of these attempted resolutions of the empiricist problem with regard to theoretical terms depended upon the ability to translate theoretical terms into an appropriate language of observation. Given that the theories in question are multiple and competing, then any adequate language of observation which might be used to arbitrate between them must be neutral with respect to those theories and therefore independent of any one. Competing theories could be tested only by first being translated, or partly translated, into the observation language. Empiricist theory tried to develop what it termed 'rules of correspondence' between theory and observation languages. Once the propositions of theory are translated into observation terms, then they are open to test against empirical observations.

Recognition of the importance of theory led to a variant of empiricism which was based on deduction rather than induction. A new orthodoxy was inaugurated by the work of Karl Popper under the title of the 'hypothetico-deductive method'. The development of scientific knowledge was held to depend on the scientists' ability to develop theories which would lead to hypotheses in any given science. Empirical consequences would than be deduced from these hypotheses, and subjected to empirical test, so that false hypotheses could be eliminated. Popper argued that science proceeded by a process of conjectures and refutations. The conjectural moment was both the moment of theory construction, and witness to human freedom and creativity. It was governed only by the limits of bold speculation and intellectual daring. The resulting hypotheses were then subject to the acid moment of empirical test, the moment of objectivity and control. Those hypotheses and theories which survived repeated attempts to refute them by the production of contrary evidence provided the most certain knowledge that we could hope to have. Knowledge, for Popper, could never be more than provisional and uncertain. It consisted in the elimination of error rather than the production of truth; refutation not verification. But the moment of empirical test remained privileged, as it had been for the positivists whom Popper attacked. It is his privileging of the empirical test which allows us to class him as an empiricist rather than a conventionalist. For at the very least, Popper had to hold that the propositions in which the results of the empirical test were couched were more certain than the propositions of the theoretical hypotheses which they tested.

Another important and influential thinker closely associated in some respects with Popper's position was Karl Hempel. He developed a formal model of scientific explanation known as the 'covering law model'. Any given phenomenon was explained when it was brought under a covering general law. As with simple empiricism, the covering law model assumes that the relationships between phenomena are regular, and that they always produce consequences at the level of sense data which are subject to empirical test. Both of these more sophisticated variants of empiricism failed to solve the problem of observation language and its relation to the terms of theory, although both have paid considerable attention to the problem and rejected simple-minded solutions. Popper in particular marks the point of transition between empiricism and conventionalism.

2. CONVENTIONALISM

i. Conventionalism and the Languages of Theory and Observation
If Popper's privileging of the propositions of the empirical test keeps him in the ranks of empiricism, his account of theory and theory construction places him with the conventionalists. It is no accident that one of the most influential contemporary conventionalists, Thomas Kuhn, stimulated a vigorous and fruitful debate between his supporters and those of Popper.

The hypothetico-deductive model of explanation recognised not only the importance of theory but its pluralism. If empirical testing was to adjudicate between competing theories, then they could not be couched in theory-dependent terms which prejudged what they purported to test. The quest for a neutral language of observation has a long history. The main thrust of the conventionalist attack on empiricism is that such a neutral observation language cannot in principle be found. Experience is never directly given, conceptless. But the concepts in terms of which experience is ordered and recorded are not and cannot be theory-neutral. Thomas Kuhn's flamboyant conventionalism declared that all languages of observation and experience are theory-impregnated. He contended that sense-perception itself depends upon theory, so that the way in which we perceive the world, the sensations and experiences we have, depend upon the theoretical presuppositions we bring to it. It follows that knowledge cannot be validated by an appeal to experience because the very terms of our experience presuppose certain knowledge-claims, and beg the questions which they are supposed to resolve. For Kuhn, the history of science is not the cumulative process, brick upon brick, of the empiricist account, in which each scientist is 'a pigmy standing on the shoulders of giants' as the falsely modest disclaimer of innumerable acknowledgement pages has it. Rather it is a succession of discontinuous 'paradigms'. Paradigms are mutually exclusive and incommensurable frames of reference, theories and methods for ordering, examining and explaining the world. Kuhn divides the history of each science into long periods of 'normal science', punctuated by briefer periods of 'revolutionary science'. In any period of 'normal science' a single paradigm will reign in a mature discipline. This ruling paradigm determines not only the concepts, theories and methods which are acceptable to the community of scientists who work within that discipline, but even what actually counts as a problem. There are no rational procedures for deposing a ruling paradigm, choosing between rivals, or installing a new one. But like dictators, each is overthrown in due course and replaced after the coup by a new despot.

ii. *Conventionalism and 'the Real'*
Kuhn goes so far as to claim not merely that different paradigms are different interpretations of reality, but that each paradigm constitutes reality anew in its own terms. Because the terms of rival paradigms are incommensurable, reality becomes a function of the paradigm, rather than something independent of all paradigms against which rival interpretations can be measured. People who use different paradigms literally live in different worlds, says Kuhn.

The limit position which all conventionalisms more or less approach is one in which the world is in effect constructed in and by theory. Given that there is no rational procedure for choosing between theories, relativism is the inevitable result. Epistemological relativism does not necessarily entail a denial that there is a real material world. But if our only access to it is via a succession of theories which describe it in mutually exclusive terms, then the concept of an independent reality ceases to have any force or function. If the first stage in the displacement of empiricism is the recognition that theories and therefore knowledge are socially produced, the second which often follows close upon its heels is the expansion of theory until it fills the world. Instead of the empiricist's instrumentalist view of theory as a tool for the production of knowledge of reality, reality in conventionalism is swallowed up by theory, and there are as many 'realities' as there are different theories of reality (or paradigms).

iii. Conventionalism and Theories of Language

It is interesting to note the similarities between conventionalism in the philosophy of science and certain developments in modern linguistics. Since Saussure's pioneering work, linguistics has placed a wedge between the terms of a language and their referents in the real world, insisting that it is not what it refers to that defines a term, but its place within the system of terms and relations which constitutes a language. In discussing Saussure's theory, Frederick Jameson notes that for Saussure:

> . . . it is the totality of systematic language which is analogous to whatever organised structures exist in the world of reality and that our understanding proceeds from one whole or gestalt to the other, rather than on a one to one basis. But of course, it is enough to present the problem in these terms *for the whole notion of reality itself to become suddenly problematic.* (Jameson, 1972, pp32–3) (my emphasis)

Like Saussurean linguistics, conventionalist accounts of theory understand the meanings of the terms of theory to be determined by their place within a system of theoretical terms. They are internally defined by the theory rather than by reference to some object in reality. Conventionalist theories of knowledge share with Saussurean linguistics a tendency to transform this real gain in the theory of linguistic *meaning* into a justification for avoiding the thorny problem of *reference*. Put in this way, the problem becomes 'how is it possible for terms which take their meaning from their place in a system of terms to refer to real objects which exist outside of that system of terms?' The problem is neatly evaded by making language in effect the only reality, or making reality a function of language. This solution is certainly available to many contemporary forms of social theory, including symbolic interactionism, ethnomethodology, and other idealisms. But it is not open to marxist materialism. Signs cannot be permitted to swallow up their referents in a never-ending chain of signification, in which one sign always points on to another, and the circle is never broken by the intrusion of that to which the sign refers.

At this point it is necessary to raise certain questions which must confront any attempt to unite marxism with modern linguistics. If marxism is a realism, then it cannot rest upon a conventionalist theory of language. Yet it is precisely this combination which informs recent developments in marxist cultural studies. There are two possible responses to this situation. The first is to attempt to reconcile marxism with conventionalism and the second is to look for a realist theory of language. Marxist cultural studies* has pursued the first alternative. This has been facilitated by the development in Althusserianism of a form of marxism which has distinct conventionalist leanings. In the last resort, Althusser himself draws back from fully fledged conventionalism. He is a realist by fiat. But he sails dangerously close to the wind, while the post-Althusserians Barry Hindess and Paul Hirst abandon caution and openly embrace conventionalism without (as yet) disavowing marxism.

3. REALISM

i. Realism, 'the Real' and 'Ontological Depth'

Modern epistemological realism accepts much of the conventionalist critique of empiricism. In particular it concedes that knowledge is socially constructed and that language, even the language of experience, is theory-impregnated. Yet it retains the empiricist insistence that the real world cannot be reduced to language or to theory, but is independent of both, and yet knowable. The task of knowledge is to produce knowledge *of* that real independent world, and not simply elegant and internally consistent constructions which endlessly refer inwards to themselves. The realist acknowledgement of the external world must be more than the empty rhetoric of a world about which nothing can be said or known: the Kantian 'thing-in-itself' which always escapes language and thought. If realism is to be more than a token gesture, then the external world which it posits must be one which is in principle accessible and about which things can be said and known.

Realism may best be characterised by a comparison with empiricism on the one hand, and conventionalism on the other, since it shares features of both. Sophisticated empiricism, the hybrid empiricism/conventionalism of the hypothetico-deductive model, looked for the *logical form* which all *bona fide* explanations shared, and found it in the form of the theoretically derived covering law. For realism no *formal* criteria can be adequate to the task of characterising scientific explanation. Many examples can be found of 'explanations' which can be formulated as covering laws but which we would not want to accept as genuine explanations at all and, vice-versa, genuine explanations which cannot be so formulated. Some regularities are — simply that — regularities: for instance, the regularity with which the sun rises and sets. We do not feel that a given instance has been explained until we know the structure of relationships which cause that regularity. Conversely, something may interfere on occasion with the operation of cause-effect

*Many of the contributions to marxist cultural studies which can be found in the work of *Screen, Working Papers in Cultural Studies, Ideaology and Consciousness*, etc. assume and contribute to a conventionalist interpretation of marxism.

relations so that no regularity can be detected, yet we want to say that the citation of that cause-effect explains the phenomenon in question. Thus when we attempt to explain single events, such as a plane crash, it is unlikely that the explanation can be immediately referred to any regularity of the form 'whenever x, then y'. This problem has led to the distinction between laws and mere empirical generalisations, and to the assertion that explanations which cannot be referred to a law simply mark gaps in our knowledge. We may not be able to explain the plane crash in terms of laws governing regular relationships, but the explanation will not be complete until we can.

Realism eschews all such *ad hoc* temporising. It argues that substantive rather than formal criteria of explanation are required. The realist Rom Harre (1972, p187) has accounted for the power of science to provide adequate explanations of phenomena in its development of theories which have what he terms 'ontological depth'. Theories develop models of real structures and processes which lie at a 'deeper' level of reality than the phenomena they are used to explain. The theory explains the phenomenon because the phenomenon and the 'deep structures' are causally connected. Thus the explanatory power of a theory resides not in the formal *logical* relationship which connects the propositions of the theory to the propositions of empirical observation, but in real *causal* connections between the different levels of the real phenomena to which the theory refers. These real connections may or may not result in empirical regularities which could be expressed in terms of a covering law.

ii. Realism and the Languages of Theory and Observation
For the realist, the entities and processes conceptualised in theories are not convenient fictions, nor summaries of empirical data, as they are for the empiricist. The terms which refer to those entities and processes therefore cannot be fully or, in some cases, even partially translated into terms with empirical referents. Reality is not, for the realist, coextensive with what can be empirically observed. But it does have effects which are open to empirical observation. It is this link between 'the real' and the 'empirical', depth and surface, which gives us access to the former and makes it possible to develop scientific knowledge. Therefore realism shares with empiricism the importance which it grants to experiment and empirical observation in the development of knowledge. But this moment of empirical test is not given the unique privilege accorded it by empiricism. For it is only theoretically informed and controlled experience which can act as a guide to 'the real'. The moment of theory is equally privileged, as it is within conventionalism. But unlike conventionalism, realism does not allow theory to englobe reality and push out any place for the empirical. It does not allow theory to expand until it fills and defines the world.

If accounting for theory is the major problem of empiricism, then accounting for the working scientist's predilection for experiment and observation is the major problem for conventionalism. If Kuhn's (or for that matter, Hindess and Hirst's) conventionalism were taken at full face value, then experiment and observation could only be viewed either as ritual games which scientists happen to play, or as the result of the scientists' philosophical naïveté. For the notion of putting theory to the test of reality makes no sense on the conventionalist interpretation of knowledge construction. The results of such 'tests' will already be contained in the theoretical presuppositions it makes in its very descriptive language.

iii. Realism, Criteria of 'the Real' and Knowledge of 'the Real'

We have seen that empiricism conflates what *is* with what can be *known* through experience. Yet claims about what is and what can be known cannot be kept entirely separate. The reality claims of realist theory would be neither here nor there unless accompanied by epistemological criteria which allow those claims to be tested against rival claims of rival theories. Empiricism is committed to some version of the correspondence theory of truth. That is to say, a proposition is held to be true if what it asserts 'corresponds' to what is the case with regard to the phenomena to which it refers. Conventionalism has no place for the idea of 'correspondence to reality' since it posits no independent reality to which its theories need to correspond. It turns instead to the rationalist criterion of *coherence* for its theory of truth. Theories, as bearers of their own reality, cannot be assessed in terms of the extent to which they 'correspond' to that reality. The order of being and of knowledge being inextricably connected for conventionalism, the 'correspondence' of theory to object is already given because the object is theoretically determined and defined. Theories and theoretically determined 'realities' can however be assessed according to their internal coherence and consistency.

Realism's criterion of truth recognises that theories must be consistent and coherent. But finally, like empiricism, realism rests upon the notion of correspondence to reality. Unlike empiricism, however, the reality to which theories correspond is not, for the realist, identical to the empirical world: the world as it exists at the level of sense data, generated through observation and experiment. The propositions of theory relate to the 'deep' ontological furniture of the universe, rather than to the surface at which experience is located. Experience, properly interpreted, gives us access to that 'deep' ontological layer because it is causally connected to it. Only when the causal connection is understood can experience act as a guide to the real.

To take a well-worn example, a stick placed in water looks bent. The theory of optics tells us why this is so. Armed with this theory, we will be able to use our observations to determine the real shape of the stick. Similarly, the exchange between capitalist and labourer in which labour-power is bought and sold has the appearance of and is experienced as an equal exchange. The labour theory of value uncovers not the 'reality' behind an 'illusion', but another, deeper level of social relations of production which explains not only why that exchange is really unequal, but also why it has the form of an equal exhange. Armed with the labour theory of value, the worker can begin to use his/her experiences of exchange and the production process as a guide to the reality of capitalism.

The major challenge to realism is to give an adequate account of 'correspondence to reality' without recourse to the empiricist chimera of a theory-neutral language of observation. Benton avoids any discussion of correspondence, but makes some useful suggestions on ways of assessing rival theories. If theories are to be assessed for their 'adequacy to the real' then we must develop some means of rational comparison between what the radical conventionalist Kuhn declares to be incommensurable — rival theories of 'reality'. Benton establishes the commensurability of theories via the following arguments:

(*a*) While objects may be described by mutually incompatible concepts which take their meanings from the different theoretical systems in which they occur, nevertheless it is sometimes possible to establish that their object of reference is the same. Difference of *meaning* does not preclude identity of *reference*. Benton places great weight upon our ability to *produce* the object of reference common to two theories and upon the existence of:

> . . . procedures for producing the substance, which may be copied, taught, learned, etc. without presupposing what is at issue between two theories. (Benton, 1977, p187)

(*b*) An objective reality is a reality common to all sciences (although different sciences may address themselves to the explanation of different 'levels' and aspects of that reality). This brings each science potentially into a relationship with all others. The history of the different sciences is one of combined and unequal development. Any single science may be supported, at any given stage of its development, by others which are more advanced. The requisite 'observation language' may be borrowed from another science. This may be illustrated by an example which is commonly cited.

The theory of planetary motion requires the use of the telescope as a test instrument when it wishes to relate theory to empirical observation. The telescope is not a theory-neutral instrument of observation, but it may be treated as such for this purpose, since the theory on which it depends — the theory of optics — is not the same as the theory which it is being used to test. Only if the theory of planetary motion itself has a stake in the theory of optics does the use of the telescope become problematic. Of course the theory which supplies the test instruments of other theories may itself be brought into question by a scientific revolution of the kind described by Kuhn. In that case the theory of planetary motion will feel the reverberations. But no revolution, in science or society, is or can be total. Not everything can be placed in question at one and the same time. Well-attested theories and results drawn from other disciplines are vital resources for any given science. They provide theoretical models, putative causal mechanisms, test instruments, and a body of well-attested 'facts' essential for cognate fields. Like socialism in one country, science in one discipline is doomed to failure. Borrowings and interconnections between disciplines are endemic in the history of science, and necessary to its development. Uneven and combined development is the law of scientific knowledge as it is of the history of social formations.

(c) A third argument is offered by Bhaskar. Even the most extreme version of conventionalism, which claims that theories are literally incommensurable, paradoxically pays testimony to the existence of a common reality. It only makes sense to speak of theories as incommensurable if they are in some sense 'about' the same thing. Hot dinners are not incommensurable with wallpaper, because there is no basis for comparison between them. The description of x as 'phlogiston' *is* incommensurable with its description as 'oxygen' because they are descriptions *of the same thing*. As Bhaskar says, it makes no sense to claim that the rules of cricket were incommensurable with the rules of chess. (But while this argument of Bhaskar's is in its own way unanswerable, it does not of course help us to determine which of two incommensurable descriptions of the same thing is to be preferred.)

(d) I have already pointed out that conventionalism can give no account of the 'game' of reality-testing played by scientists who persist in wishing to test their theories. Yet it is this game which is Kuhn's whole motor of scientific progress and change. It is in the attempt to test theories that anomalies, results that do not fit the theories, are thrown up, and it is when anomalies have accumulated to an embarrassing extent, or to the point when the scientists' careers are blocked by their inability to solve the problems posed within the paradigm used by the theory, that the decisive shift from 'normal' to 'revolutionary' science takes place. The coherence theory of truth, and a theory-determined 'reality' cannot explain how it comes about that there are anomalies between theory and 'reality'. Anomalies testify to the existence of a real world which is independent of theory but which theory explains, more or less adequately. Only realism can give an account of the actual history of science, and of the possibility of progress through revolution.*

*I am indebted for this point to Phil Fryer's comments on the ms.

To sum up: realism is both an ontology and an epistemology. It makes assertions about the nature of the real world, and these assertions have consequences for the manner in which that world may be known (or if you will, in which knowledge of the world may be produced). It does not identify the real with what can be experienced, but as a multi-layered structure, consisting of entities and processes lying at different levels of that structure, including the surface level of the empirical world. The empirical world with which we are familiar is causally connected to 'deeper' ontological levels, and it is by virtue of these causal connections that we can use sense-data, experience and observation in constructing knowledge of the structures and processes of the real. These causal connections cannot themselves be understood through experience, because neither the underlying structures nor the connection between these structures and the empirical world are themselves experienced. The connection can only be reconstructed in knowledge. But these connections are vital for the realist theory of knowledge. Experience may be a treacherous and misleading guide to the structures of the real when unassisted by theory. On the other hand theories are mere flights of fancy unless they retain their link to the world of experience. The relationship between theory and experience is not however circular, because of the interconnection between different theories of connected aspects of a common reality and the manner in which one theory draws upon the resources provided by another, collectively generating a residue of theoretically grounded 'observations' which may be taken as the testing ground for any given theory at any given point in time. The 'combined and unequal development' of disciplines is necessary to the grounding of any one. Without this necessary point of contact outside its own theoretically defined field, individual disciplines are condemned to the circularity described by Kuhn.

4. MARXISM IS A REALISM

i. Marxism and its Object of Reference

A theory may be a realist theory and yet be false. There may be more than one realist theory of a given phenomenon which explains it in quite different ways. Here I am not concerned with the question of the truth or validity of marxism as a theory of society and history, but only with its credentials as a realist theory.

Marxism has, of course, been interpreted in other terms throughout its long history. It has had positivist interpreters, who need not detain us. Of more interest are recent conventionalist marxisms, such as that of Barry Hindess and Paul Hirst. Conventionalists such as Hindess and Hirst do not make a distinction between positivism and realism, but interpret empiricism broadly to include both. I shall argue here that the conventionalist interpretation of marxism leads to the loss of what is most useful and distinctive in it, while the realist interpretation brings out what is most valuable in Marx's work.

'Marxisms' of every complexion, from the positivism of Kautsky, through the humanism of Lukács, to the anti-humanism of Althusser, are agreed upon the first principle of realism: that there exists an objective and independent social world, which can be known. It is this premise which has been abandoned by conventionalism in favour of a 'reality' which to all intents and purposes is constructed through theory, since the real world outside of theory cannot be known, cannot be compared with the world posited by theory. It is true, *pace* Kuhn and the conventionalists, that that real, concrete world can only be known and described within the terms of some theory or another. And it is true that different theories demarcate the world in quite different terms. But while this makes *knowledge* of the world theory-dependent, it does not make the world itself theory-dependent, nor does it follow that a world independent of theory cannot be known through theory. This only follows when the connection between theories and their real referents is severed, as it is within conventionalism. Here Benton's point about the importance of maintaining a clear distinction between the meaning of a term and its referent must be remembered. It is true that classical political economy and marxism differ in their descriptions and explanations of capitalism, and that the terms in which they cast their theories and explanations are drawn from mutually exclusive systems of ideas. It does not follow that the term 'capitalism' refers to something entirely different in each case. It may demarcate boundaries differently, but the object of reference of marxism and political economy are one and the same. Although the 'production' of capitalist social relations presents problems of a different order to the 'production' of phlogiston/oxygen, nevertheless assuming that such social experiments were possible, political economists and marxists would produce *the same thing* under different descriptions.

ii. Marxism, Experience and the Empirical

Marx makes the realist assertion of the necessity to go beyond appearances, beyond the manner in which social relations are experienced, in order to arrive at knowledge of those social relations: 'science would be superflous if there was an immediate coincidence of the appearance and reality of things.' (Marx, in Lukács, 1970, p26) He does not identify the real with the empirical. Appearances, taken at face value, are misleading. They can only be understood in the light of the theory of historical materialism. But as a realist Marx makes a causal link between experience/appearances and those objects and relations in the real social world which they are appearances *of*. Althusser places a wedge between the two by arguing that experience/appearances are produced only as a result of 'ideological practice', which is in turn only determined by the social relations of production in the 'last instance'. Hindess and Hirst sever this slender connection altogether, so that the ideological practice which determines experience, including the individual's experience of his/her social identity, becomes a fully autonomous practice, limited only by its 'conditions of existence' in other practices of the social formation. But for both the moderate Althusser and the radical Hindess and Hirst, the effect of this separation of the ideological from the economic is to pre-empt any role for experience in knowledge production, as we shall see in the next chapter when their theories are examined in more detail. Experience can, as a result, only provide a guide to ideological production, and not to the real structure of social relationships.

iii. Marxism and the Language of Theory

By contrast, Marx's theory of commodity fetishism makes a direct link between the forms of the social relations of production under capitalism, and the appearances which these relations have for individuals and groups who experience them. Under the system of capitalist commodity production social relations take the form of relationships between things. This form of social relations therefore gives rise to appearances which are misleading when taken at face value. If human agents order their experience and activities in terms of these appearances, they will fail to develop knowledge of the reality of capitalist social relations. Marx uses the concept of commodity fetishism to explain the way in which capitalism is experienced, since he sees experience as a function of the position of human agents within the ensemble of social relations, and the objective form which those social relations take within the mode of production in question.

This theory of commodity fetishism allows Marx to answer the question of the source of ideology. Ideologies are defined as those theories which take the appearances of social relations under capitalism at face value. This is at least a minimal criterion for distinguishing ideology from adequate knowledge. Knowledge is a function of the development of theories which explain the appearances or forms of capitalist social relations in terms of the real underlying structures and processes of capitalism — the social relations which these appearances are appearances of.

This leaves open the further question of the source of ideological and scientific theories. Here the orthodox answer is to relate the development of ideas to class interest and the class struggle. This allows us to add to the above minimal definition of ideology. For it is the bourgeoisie which is the class in whose interest it is to develop theories of capitalism which take the appearances or forms of capitalist social relations at full face value, naturalising them as eternal and necessary forms; while it is the proletariat which, if it is to overthrow capitalism in pursuit of its collective class interests, must develop adequate knowledge of the reality of capitalist social relations and the 'laws of motion' of capitalism.

This answer, further developed in the work of Lukács, leaves certain questions unanswered. It does not, for example, tell us anything about the work of theory construction, whether the theory in question is ideological or scientific. In drawing attention to this work, and attempting to analyse its processes, Althusser has made a valuable intervention. For class interest does not lead automatically to theory construction, and neither do the forms of capitalist social relations automatically generate the terms and concepts of ideological theories which have tried to explain them. It does, however, indicate the point of view from which the work of knowledge construction must take place — the point of view of the proletariat, in its struggle with capitalism. I shall examine in the next chapter the difficulties which Althusser's theory of ideology and knowledge construction creates for theorising the role of this collective class subject of history.

iv. Marxism and the Human Subject

The Althusserian and post-Althusserian criticism of Lukács, that he failed to problematise the individual human subject of experience (Hirst, 1976), applies to Marx as well as to Lukács, in respect of his theory of commodity fetishism. Marx provides no account of the individual human subject and the manner in which it is constituted. This is not necessarily a telling objection however, for Marx leaves the space for a theory of the subject. Unlike empiricism, realism does not depend upon positing a knowing subject which is given rather than socially constructed. But it is absolutely essential that any such theory of the social constitution of the subject should not sever the connection between that (constituted) subject, experience and knowledge after the manner of conventionalism, by severing the connection between the representation of experience and the real objects which they are representations of.

5. MARXISM IS A (HISTORICAL) MATERIALISM

i. Materialism

Realism does not uniquely define marxism as a social theory. It does not even serve to separate idealism from materialism, since there are several forms of 'objective idealism' which are fully realist in their epistemologies, although the reality they posit is non-material.

Materialism is a term which has suffered considerable loss of definition in recent years. It has become almost interchangeable with 'real'. This is partly the result of changes within the natural sciences, always 'opinion leaders' in these matters. The eighteenth-century model of physical reality was a mechanist one. The material world was thought to consist in atomic particles of matter, mechanically coming into contact with one another and setting up an endless chain of causation, like Hume's billiard balls. Even at its height, the atomic/mechanist model had difficulties with concepts thrown up within the most prestigious sciences, such as the concept of gravity as a force acting at a distance, without direct physical contact. Since Einstein's revolution, the atomic/mechanist model has become increasingly obsolete. The concept of the 'material' has had to be elastic enough to include the furniture of contemporary physics, things which are very far removed from the tangible objects previously connoted by 'material'. This redefining of the material world in the physical sciences has been systematic and disciplined. While it is true that many things are now included under the concept which were previously excluded, the development of the sciences themselves provide the context for this extension of 'material'. But it has had radical consequences elsewhere. The flood-gates have been opened. For if the natural sciences can get away with the *coup* of redefining as material anything which their theories designate as real, then why not the social sciences also? Materialism is the claim that what is material has causal primacy. If it is redefined so that anything which claims to be real also qualifies for the label 'material', then materialism becomes empty. The way is cleared for theorists in such disparate fields as para-psychology and the history of ideas to claim that the objects designated in their theories are real and therefore material, and that their theories are materialist.

The resurgence of marxism in the social sciences in recent years has been associated with a return to fashion of materialist claims. Its new-found popularity has been at the expense of any real content. It would be neither appropriate nor helpful here to enter into any general discussion of materialism. All that is needed is a specification of the meaning which must be retained if the notion of a materialist conception of history is to have any specificity.

Firstly, it is not helpful to use 'material' and 'real' interchangeably. Materialism is more usefully restricted to an assertion of the relationship between different levels of reality, when reality is conceived on the realist model of a multi-layered structure with different levels, or depths. Thus to assert that ideas are real is perfectly proper, but to try to define ideas as a *material* reality leads only to confusion; while to assert the primacy of ideas is to attack materialism. Marxism is a materialism which consists in the principle of the primacy of the mode of production, within the social formation. The mode of production, in Harre's terms, has greater 'ontological depth' than the other layers of the social formation which it is used to explain. Given the current debasement of the term 'production' in marxist theory, it is necessary to add that 'mode of production' here carries the sense which it had for Marx in *Capital* — the mode of production (and reproduction) of material life. It does not refer to a generalised concept which is applicable to the production of ideas, for instance, or for that matter, individual human subjects. The primacy of the mode of production is an indispensable principle of marxist materialism, that which distinguishes it finally from other realist theories of society and history.

ii. Marxism and History

The second point which must be insisted upon, and which has been abandoned in conventionalist marxism, is that marxism is a theory of history. It cannot be transformed into a theory of some static 'social formation' in the manner of sociological structural-functionalism. Conventionalist theories of science tend to transform their 'objects' into closed systems which are self-reproducing. This is a direct consequence of the conflation within conventionalism of the real with the objects of theory.

The capitalist mode of production is an object which is theoretically defined within marxist theory, and which does not as such correspond exactly with any real society found in history. Nevertheless it *refers* to real social relationships which exist in historical societies, and which explain aspects of their development. The theory of the capitalist mode of production developed by Marx investigates the 'powers' of that mode of production to produce certain specific effects, including certain kinds of experience. As it is specified within the theory, the capitalist mode of production is a system which is artificially isolated, rather in the manner of scientific models, in order to discover the relationship between its parts. It is closed only in the sense that the effects of various things which in reality might interfere in the operation of cause-effect between its parts, are excluded from the model, the better to investigate those cause-effect relations. It is emphatically *not* closed in the sense used in modern systems theory. It is not a self-reproducing system in equilibrium, even in splended theoretical isolation, let alone in reality. Indeed, an essential part of Marx's theory of the capitalist mode of production is its dynamic openness — it cannot be self-reproducing because it generates conflicting requirements for its own reproduction.

Some conventionalists argue that history is not a proper object of scientific knowledge, whether the history of the physical or the social world. They argue that historical events are the outcome of a number of quite different causal sequences interacting with one another in any given conjuncture. Each of these causal sequences will be the proper study of one or another specialist science, and there cannot be a single theory which will incorporate all of them and which can be used to explain or predict historical change. Historical events can therefore only be analysed, using these specialist sciences, and are not proper subjects of scientific explanation and theory. Even the realist Bhaskar comes close to ceding history to analysis rather than to science. He argues that scientific disciplines operate by carving out some 'relatively autonomous' area of determinations, and proceed by building models of the real structures and processes which produce these determinations. It is necessary to study these 'relatively autonomous' areas of determination in isolation from each other in the first instance, before their relative weight and effect in 'open systems' can be known. History is such an open system, in which a variety of radically different types of determination come into play so that the outcome is always contingent and uncertain. These different determinations are the proper study of specialist disciplines and independent sciences. Historians must draw upon the findings of these disciplines in constructing historical analyses of particular 'conjunctures'.

Yet marxism is precisely the study of what happens in history, and cannot be parcelled out to independent areas of investigation. Its materialism consists in the principle that of the various 'powers' at play in the social world those of the mode of production have primacy. It follows that the study of the other different kinds of social determination (e.g. the social determinants of the production of individual human subjects, or of literary forms) *must always be studied within the context of a given mode of production.* This is a minimal definition of marxist materialism, and it draws attention to what, for better or worse, gives marxism its distinctiveness as a theory of the social world and history. Without this principle, marxism becomes indistinguishable from either functionalist interactionism or a Weberian sociology of types.

CHAPTER 2

Louis Althusser

In this country, the most consistent attempt to develop a conventionalist marxism is to be found in the work of Barry Hindess and Paul Hirst, the outcome of a critical engagement with Althusser. While their own work has centred elsewhere, Hindess and Hirst have had considerable influence on marxist cultural studies. At the present time marxist cultural studies divides between those who have welcomed Hindess and Hirst's work for its congruence with conventionalist theories of language, and those who have drawn back from some of its implications. Common to both groups is an interest in the language, 'discourse' or 'signifying practice' of cultural production, and in the 'ideological effects' which such 'discourse' produces. The point of separation between them comes over the complete substitution of discourse analysis for analysis of social reality. Discourse analysis is never far from the temptation of treating social reality itself as a discursive order, rather than as a reality external to discourse but to which discourse refers.

There is evidence then of a certain withdrawal from conventionalism in marxist cultural studies recently. But this has usually stopped short of withdrawal from Althusser's work, and his theory of ideology remains the backbone of marxist cultural studies. In this chapter I want to explore the extent to which Althusser's own framework is implicated in conventionalism, in order that the extent of the reappraisal which will be necessary if marxist cultural studies is to return to marxist materialism and realism may be appreciated.

Althusser constructs his interpretation of Marx against 'empiricist', 'historicist' and 'humanist' readings. He defines empiricism as the belief that knowledge is something which can be abstracted from the real world, and known through experience. Humanism is the view that 'man is the measure of all things'; that the social world is constructed by men and women, even if they do so under conditions not of their choosing, and without full consciousness of what they do.

In Benton and in Keat and Urry, Althusser's interpretation of Marx is used to establish their thesis that marxism is a realism. Despite this, I shall argue here that much of Althusser's work is inconsistent with realism, and that it contains strong elements of conventionalism whose effects are far reaching.

Althusser shares in common with the humanism he opposes a concern to rescue marxism from the economism of the period of the second International. But he sees the humanist resolution as merely the obverse side of the same coin. It turns economism on its head, but shares the same 'problematic'. To understand this we must begin with the base/superstructure metaphor, which expressed that problematic. This is premised, it is argued, upon a mind/matter dualism shared by both economism and idealist humanism. Ideas are seen as reflections, distorted or otherwise, of material reality. Althusser, in *For Marx* and *Reading Capital*, proposes a redefinition of the social formation as what he terms a 'structure in dominance'. The social formation consists, he argues, in a series of 'material practices' which are mutually interdependent. Each practice is relatively autonomous, both determined and determining within the whole of which it is a part. Althusser defines 'practice' as:

> . . . the *transformation* of a determinate given raw material into a determinate *product*, a transformation effected by determinate human labour, using determinate means (of production). (Althusser, 1977a, p166)

He identifies, in *For Marx*, four such practices (or levels): the economic, political, ideological and theoretical. While each of these practices has its own specific effectivity within the whole, they are not always and everywhere equally effective.

Each practice has its own particular contradictions, which are not mere reflections or expressions of the contradictions of the economic level. At any given moment, the contradictions of one level will play the dominant role in determining the outcome of the historical conjuncture:

> . . . in real history determination in the last instance by the economy is exercised precisely in the permutations of the principal role between the economy, politics, theory, etc. (ibid., p213)

The economic level, in all social formations, retains only this privilege of determination in a last instance which never comes:

> . . . the economic dialectic is never active *in the pure state;* in History, these instances, the superstructures, etc. — are never seen to step respectfully aside when their work is done or, when the Time comes, as his pure phenomena, to scatter before His Majesty the Economy as he strides along the royal road of the Dialectic. From the first moment to the last, the lonely hour of the 'last instance' never comes. (Althusser, 1977, p113)

The economic level is determining, argues Althusser, in the sense that the mode of production of a given social formation determines which of the levels of that formation shall be dominant, what its 'degree of effectivity' shall be. The economic determines by a process of delegation of effectivity to other levels:

> . . . the nature of the relations of production not only calls for or does not call for a certain form of superstructure but also establishes the *degree of effectivity* delegated to a certain level of the social totality. (Althusser and Balibar, 1977, p177)*

In his substitution of this ensemble of practices, under the delegatory guidance of the economic, for the base/superstructure hierarchy, Althusser breaks with the dualism of ideas/material forces. What distinguishes one level from another is not its materiality. All levels are constituted by practices, and all practices are material, just as all are informed by ideas. The practices are differentiated by their different functions and effects within the totality. Both the ideological and the theoretical are redefined as practices which produce particular products and, as such, are as much material forces as are economic or political practices.

2. ALTHUSSER'S THEORY OF KNOWLEDGE: CONVENTIONALIST OR REALIST?

Althusser's theory of knowledge rests on his general concept of practice, or production. Knowledge is the end product of a specific practice. It is not something inscribed in the real and abstracted from it through experience.

i. Knowledge Production: the 'Problematic'

This key concept in Althusser's theory of knowledge has certain similarities to Kuhn's 'paradigm'. It refers to a whole system of interrelated and mutually defined concepts and problems. The problematic of a theory goes beyond the questions it knowingly imposes, to those which are absent, but structuring of the problematic nevertheless. The problematic is buried below the surface of the text, to be uncovered, like the Freudian unconscious, by a 'symptomatic reading' analogous to the analyst's reading of slips of the tongue, errors and dreams. To determine the problematic of a text it is necessary to put to it 'the

---

*Balibar takes up this idea of delegated determination in his analysis of feudalism. He argues that under feudal production, the direct producer retains possession of the major means of production. Hence the surplus must be extracted by extra-economic compulsions of a legal and coercive nature, emanating, according to Balibar, from the political level of the feudal social formation. (Althusser and Balibar, 1977, pp219–24)

question of its questions'. As with Kuhn's paradigm, the concept of the problematic yields a history of ideas which emphasises breaks and discontinuities. For Kuhn, these breaks punctuated the whole history of a discipline, and are in principle unending. For Althusser the crucial break occurs at the moment when a science is founded. This 'epistemological break' (a concept culled from Gaston Bachelard) marks the distance between a science and the ideological problematic from which that science has broken. It may be crossed by apparent continuities. The same term may occur within both ideological and scientific problematics. 'Alienation' occurs occasionally in Marx's mature writings which Althusser holds to be scientific, as well as in the 'pre-marxist' early works which belong to an ideological problematic taken from Feuerbach. This duplication of terms occurs because, in the moment of transition from ideology to science, attempts are being made to say new things within the framework of an old problematic within which they cannot strictly be said. And in any case, the continuities are more apparent than real. The term may be the same, but the concept which the term denotes will be different. This is because the meaning of a concept is a function of its place among all the concepts of the problematic in which it occurs, and, by definition, the two problematics which share the common term are different.

A scientific problematic, like Kuhn's paradigm, circumscribes the work of knowledge production within a discipline. Althusser applies his general definition of practice to the practice of knowledge production. The raw materials of that production are the received notions of a given field of enquiry. Initially these will exist as ideological notions contained in common sense. These raw materials are referred to by Althusser as *Generalities I*. They exist, he insists, only in thought. The raw materials of knowledge production are not, then, 'facts' or states of affairs in the world, as they are for the empiricist, but ideological concepts and propositions. These raw materials are worked on and transformed during the 'production process'. The means of production are provided by the problematic, according to the existing state of theory and method. These tools of intellectual production include a conceptual framework, theory, methodological rules, etc. These Althusser calls *Generalities II*. They are applied to the raw materials of *Generalities I*, and the result, the end product, is knowledge. This has the form of 'the concrete-in-thought' which he also calls *Generalities III*.

ii. Knowledge, the Object of Knowledge, and the 'Real': the Problem of Relativism
The 'concrete-in-thought' is, in Althusser 's terminology, both the end product of knowledge production, and the 'object of knowledge'. It exists entirely within thought. However, to avoid falling into relativism or subjectivism Althusser posits in addition a real world which exists outside of thought, duplicating the object world constructed in theory.

This 'real-concrete' world is independent of thought, and untouched by it. But the production of matching 'thought-objects' allows the 'real-concrete' to be 'appropriated in thought'.

Althusser argues that the classical questions of epistemology are rendered obsolete when knowledge is understood as production. He substitutes instead the following question:

> By what mechanism does the process of knowledge, which takes place entirely in thought, produce the cognitive appropriation of its real object, which exists outside of thought? (Althusser and Balibar, 1977, p56)

This is, of course, the question posed by any realist epistemology, as we saw in the last chapter. Unfortunately Althusser provides no answer to it. Benton suggests that he cannot, because of the terms in which he poses it.

Althusser's claim that through the production of 'the concrete-in-thought' the 'real-concrete' may be appropriated might be mistaken for a tortuous expression of the correspondence theory of truth. But Althusser specifically refuses this interpretation. He argues that theories are not true because they explain the real, rather they are able to explain the real because they are true. Knowledge carries its own guarantees:

> Theoretical practice is . . . its own criterion, and contains within itself definite protocols with which to validate the quality of its product, i.e. the criteria of scientificity of the products of scientific practice . . . It has been possible to apply Marx's theory with success because it is 'true': it is not true because it has been applied with success. (ibid., p59)

This account of scientific theory escapes relativism only by virtue of the dogmatic assertion that 'the concrete-in-thought' is adequate to the real. We are not even told what would count as 'applying a theory with success'. Many mutually conflicting theories claim 'adequacy to the real' and it is difficult to imagine any theory refusing this claim when it is so cheaply made, in the absence of any requirement to produce independent criteria for evaluating rival claims. Benton points out that Althusser's 'real-concrete' has no function in his epistemology. It has, he says:

> . . . as an epistemological device the same defects as the Kantian 'thing-in-itself'. It is something about which by definition nothing can be said. Therefore we can never know what the relationship is between it and the 'concrete-in-thought' . . . The independence of the real world is asserted but cannot be asserted consistently with the rest of the theory. (Benton, 1977, p186)

This problem of the relationship between theories and the real world which they are theories *of* is, as we have seen, not peculiar to Althusser but common to all realist epistemologies. It is a problem, however, which cannot be swept aside by spurious claims to have moved beyond epistemology. Classical epistemology may have failed to provide satisfactory solutions, but the questions it raised are still relevant to contemporary theories and practices of knowledge production: questions of truth, validity, and reference.

If the 'real-concrete' is eliminated from Althusser's theory of knowledge production, then it at once becomes conventionalist. Benton notes some of the similarities between Althusser's and Kuhn's theories of knowledge. They are by no means identical, even after the removal of Althusser's 'real-concrete'. Benton himself tries to rescue Althusser for realism through his account of reference, and of the *production* of the real-concrete itself, and not just of the 'concrete-in-thought' (see p20). Unfortunately this account is incompatible with certain other aspects of Althusser's theory which Benton ignores. In particular, it is incompatible with Althusser's elimination of any place for the knowing subject and experience in the production of knowledge. This is rooted in Althusser's theory of 'ideology in general', based on his appropriation of Lacanian psychoanalysis, and it is to Althusser's concept and theory of ideology that we must now turn.

iii. Scientific Theory and Theoretical Ideologies
If Althusser fails to ground the scientificity of science in its ability to produce thought-objects which are 'adequate to the real', then he has left only one recourse, and that is to provide clear and adequate criteria whereby the distinct *practices* of knowledge production and ideology production may be identified and distinguished. He must provide criteria for demarcating science and ideology. Althusser offers at least three criteria:

(a) Science is counter-intuitive, ideology is 'obvious'. Common sense, for Althusser, is ideological and common sense is, by definition, what is 'obvious'. But science is not obvious. It is often highly counter-intuitive. Ideology relies on experience for its 'truths', and this is the reason why its truths appear obvious. Obviousness is a function of recognition by appeal to experience. Science relies not on experience but on theory for its truths. Hence the knowledge which is produced is not obvious because it does not depend on returning to experience what experience already 'knows' and can therefore recognise. Ideology depends upon this circular recognition which results when what is taken from experience is returned to it. Science, unlike ideology, does not require validation through recognition.

This criterion, or a similar one, is used, on occasion, it is true, by Marx. But there are many bodies of thought, which purport to have the status of science but which Althusser would wish to label ideologies, which are every bit as counter-intuitive as marxism, or for that matter, modern physics. Some of them might even qualify as nonsense. They can be opaque, turgid, and far, far removed from common sense. It would be invidious to name names but we can all no doubt supply our own examples. While science is certainly counter-intuitive, it does not follow that anything which is counter-intuitive is science, and therefore counter-intuitiveness alone cannot be used to distinguish science from ideology.

(b)Science is open, ideology is closed. This second criterion fares no better than the first. For while it may characterise the difference between some systems of thought which we accept as scientific, and others which we accept to be ideological, it does not always do so. Some of the most powerful ideologies do not depend upon logical closure, but on the contrary their very open-endedness is their great strength. Christianity, for instance, and probably most of the great world religions, cannot be described as a logically closed system of thought. Yet religion is, for Althusser, one of the chief 'ideological state apparatuses'. On the other hand, recent studies of the actual history of science (such as those of Kuhn and others) as opposed to idealised 'rational reconstructions' of their logic, strongly suggest that the much vaunted 'openness' of science is itself an ideology with which the scientific community protects itself and its practices, rather than a description of those practices or even of the norms which govern them. The kinds of circular reasoning which characterise closed systems of thought are found time and again in the history of *bona fide* sciences whose right to that title has never been challenged.

(c) Science draws its problems from theory: ideology from extra-theoretical sources. Benton accepts this third criterion offered by Althusser that while what counts as a problem is determined by theory in science, in ideology it is determined by practical and even political considerations.

Again this differentiation does not clearly separate every case. While the relationship between pure science and practical problems may be remote at certain stages in the history of certain sciences, in other sciences and at other times they have been very close. This is particularly the case in the social sciences, and marxism has traditionally prided itself on its close relationship with (revolutionary) practice.* Conversely Parsonian sociology generates the following problem: 'why is it that the child has two parents while the analysand has only one analyst?' Whether or not Parson's sociology counts as science or ideology, few would want to claim that this is a 'problem' which is recognisable as such outside the confines of his theory. It is neither a practical problem, nor

*I do not want to take issue on the question of whether marxism is or is not a science. Marx and Engels themselves had no doubt that it was, but even if this claim is not entered, marxists still need and wish to differentiate their work from 'bourgeois ideology'.

one which 'common sense' indicates or recognises.

What Althusser wishes to include under the label 'ideology' is extremely broad. It ranges from common-sense truisms, to theoretical systems of the order of complexity of Parsons's general theory of action. The distance which separates theoretical ideologies from common sense is far greater than that which separates them from scientific theories. Yet Althusser makes it easy to establish apparently marked differences between science and ideology by the simple expedient of comparing like with unlike: theoretical science with the truisms of common sense, rather than with theoretical ideologies which they are much closer to. The differentiation of theoretical ideologies from scientific theories is a much more formidable task, yet in the absence of criteria adequate to this task Althusser's whole project suffers and the spectre of conventionalist relativism cannot be laid.

iv. The Post-Althusserians

The narrowness of the gap which separates Althusser from conventionalism is emphasised by its final closure in the work of the post-Althusserians Barry Hindess and Paul Hirst. They develop their position out of a critique of Althusser in which the inconsistencies and contradictions of the latter have been ruthlessly eliminated. The first casualty is the 'real-concrete'. Now while I have argued that this concept is, as Benton suggests, functionless in Althusser's work, it nevertheless kept Althusser tenuously and inconsistently within the ranks of the realists, and in touch with history. This is why Hindess and Hirst's rigorous logic has the effect, often noted, of reducing Althusser to absurdity. I do not have the space here for a full consideration of their work, but I will attempt a brief sketch.

In their auto-critique, *Mode of Production and Social Formation*, Hindess and Hirst's quarrel with Althusser, and with their own former selves of *Pre-Capitalist Modes of Production*, is that he (and they) did not make a clean enough break with empiricism. In retaining the concept of the 'real-concrete' which could be appropriated by the 'concrete-in-thought'. Althusser gave, they claim, hostages to empiricism and to classical epistemology. Classical epistemology, in all its variants, is, they claim, premised upon a distinction between 'a realm of discourse on the one hand, and a realm of actual or potential objects of discourse on the other'. (Hindess and Hirst, 1977, p19) They reject any positing of two realms which are in some way correlated, and with impeccable logic they conclude:

> . . . it is then no longer possible to refer to objects existing *outside* of discourse as the measure of validity of discourse. On the contrary, in the absence of such extra-discursive (and yet specifiable) objects, the entities specified in discourse must be referred to solely in and through

the forms of discourse in which they are constituted. (ibid.)

Hindess and Hirst do not deny the existence of an external world. But it is a world about which in principle nothing can be said or known, and to which therefore the discursive practices, whether of science or ideology, cannot be referred. It cannot be used to validate those discourses. The validity of a discourse is, it follows, a matter entirely internal to that discourse itself. Since the objects of discourse exist only in and through the discourse and not in any extra-discursive realm, it also follows that there can be no communication across discourses. The objects which are posited in one discourse cannot be used to criticise another discourse in which they have no place:

> . . . Talcott Parsons has been criticised for his alleged failure to conceptualise such 'realities' as 'social change', 'social conflict' . . . and 'bourgeois' historians and social scientists have been criticised for their failure to recognise the objects specified in marxist discourse, and so on . . . This mode of analysis merely measures the substantive distance between the objects specified in one discourse and those specified in another. (ibid., p14)

The correct procedure, they claim, for dealing with any discourse is not to confront that discourse with the objects of another discourse, but to subject it to an immanent critique, for its internal inconsistencies and contradictions. It is perhaps worth spelling out through another example the consequences of this discursive relativism, taken at face value (which fortunately Hindess and Hirst do not and cannot do in their own substantive work). A history of the Third Reich which made no mention of the murder of six million Jews would be felt by most people to be seriously inadequate. Is this only because we are erroneously comparing this discourse about the Third Reich with other discourses which happen to contain among their objects 'extermination camps', 'gas chambers', 'pogroms' etc? Or is it because such discourses and their objects are quite properly referred to a world of real objects in which these things really existed, and not just internally to their own logic? I suggest that it is just as absurd to imagine that such well-attested phenomena as social change, conflict, etc. are merely 'objects of discourse' and not objects against which the adequacy of discourses is measured. What differentiates realism from this absurdly consistent conventionalism is precisely its insistence that, while concepts draw their meaning from their place within a system of concepts, these concepts can and do *refer* to real objects in a real world, about which things can be said and known.

Hindess and Hirst argue that the only discourse about social formations which meets the criterion of full internal coherence (the only criterion we have the right to require of a discourse) is their own, developed out of Althusser's model of 'structures in dominance'. This discourse posits, instead of Althusser's 'relatively autonomous practices' under the delegatory guidance of the economic, a number of absolutely autonomous practices under no delegatory guidance whatsoever, each with its own history, its own specific effects on other practices, and its own conditions of existence in other practices. There can be no question of comparing these discursive objects, the various 'economic', 'political' and 'ideological practices' of Hindess and Hirst's Social Formation Discourse, with real objects outside that discourse which, although in strict logic we cannot even name them, we may for convenience label economic, political and ideological activities. All we can ask of the objects of Hindess and Hirst's discourse is 'what are their conditions of existence, and what are their consequences?' It is, however, an absolutely pointless question, because it can have no possible bearing on what political and practical decisions and actions people take. Anyone who tried to make his/her actions conform to the 'lessons' of Hindess and Hirst's, or anyone else's, discourse would simply have failed to understand that discourse has no relationship whatsoever to an extra-discursive world of action, and therefore lessons to give. It may have *effects*, but these cannot of course, be known since the attempt to know them takes us back from the realm of cause-effect, into the realm of (another) discourse.

The consequence of drawing up this impenetrable barrier between discourse and social reality is that all real, practical activity in and on the world is rendered blind. This position cannot logically generate any politics, only a political discourse, whose effects cannot be gauged. It can only show the irrationality of all political activity, which can never be anything more than whistling in the dark. Paradoxically the only politics which is possible from this position is a complete voluntarism, in which the political act is a pure act of will which owes nothing to reason, or on the other hand a fatalistic determinism. In either case there is no point in developing political theory as an attempt to guide political action.

It is most important that marxist cultural studies, when tempted to follow the path marked out by Hindess and Hirst, should be quite clear as to where it leads. Its absurdities are more obvious when the 'object' of discourse is social formations and history, than when it is used in connection with television programmes, novels, films, etc. Here conventionalism is undeniably attractive at first sight, in its insistence that these objects are in themselves real; that they are 'discursive' or 'signifying' practices and not just passive reflectors of a given external reality. But conventionalism is no more viable as an epistemology for the construction of knowledge of cultural production than it is for the production of knowledge of the social world. However the backtracking which has already begun in respect of Hindess and Hirst's conventionalism in marxist cultural studies* cannot in my view stop short of the source of that conventionalism in Althusser's work. There is, naturally enough, a deep reluctance to recognise the extent of what will have to be discarded or rethought in recent marxist cultural studies. For an immense amount of intellectual labour has been invested in this work, and such reassessments are at best painful. It is hardly surprising if so far the work of demolition and reconstruction and the rescue of what is viable and valuable has been postponed in favour of piecemeal modification.

3. ALTHUSSER'S THEORY OF IDEOLOGY: THE PLACE OF THE SUBJECT

Althusser attempted, then, to overcome the ideas/matter dualism by positing a social formation consisting of a series of levels constituted by different practices. This entailed a shift in conceptualisations of knowledge and ideology. These were no longer to be seen as bodies of ideas which reflected other practices, but as themselves practices which were just as material as other practices and which produced specific effects, namely 'the knowledge effect' and 'the ideological effect' respectively.

i. 'Ideology in General' and the Constituted Subject

Althusser made a distinction between 'particular ideologies' and 'ideology in general'. Particular ideologies are the historically developed ideological instruments of class rule. Consistent with his general emphasis on practice, he draws attention to the ideological institutions within which ideological production takes place under capitalism — the family, school, church, mass media. He refers to them collectively as 'ideological state apparatuses'. (Althusser, 1977b) At this point, his work is heavily indebted to Gramsci. Like Gramsci, he distinguishes between particular ideologies located in common-sense thinking and those which take more abstract, systematised forms. In the preceding section of this chapter I discussed his failure to provide adequate criteria for distinguishing particular theoretical ideologies from scientific theories. I now want to turn to the problems raised by his theory of 'ideology in general'.

Ideology in general does not exist, claims Althusser, independently of particular ideologies, but is the form which all particular ideologies take. Unlike particular ideologies therefore, ideology in general is a-historical and universal, or effectively so. Unlike the state, ideology will never wither away. The universal form of all ideology is identified in its effects — that of constituting individual human beings as subjects. Before proceeding any further I want to point to a sleight of hand which has already been achieved, and which results from Althusser's having

*This may be seen in some recent issues of *Screen Education*. For example, see the article by Tony Stevens on Realism in issue No. 26, Spring 1978.

stretched the concept of ideology to cover too much. As we have seen, it includes, at the level of particular ideologies, a range of bodies of ideas, from common sense to systematic theory; and at a general level, all of these function to constitute individual human beings as subjects, and to reproduce the social order. But in his discussion of 'ideology in general', Althusser focusses only on a restricted range of ideological phenomena, namely those 'lived' ideologies that are so deeply imbued with common-sense thinking. Again he would find it much more challenging to make his case with respect to more abstract, systematised bodies of ideological thought, and it must remain doubtful whether the most important difference between, say, political economy and marxism lies in the manner in which they constitute individual human beings as subjects.

The concept of the subject is central to Althusser's theory of ideology in general. He argues that successive sciences have displaced the subject from the privileged position it occupied in classical epistemology. It was rapidly displaced from the centre of the physical world by the natural sciences, and Marx and Freud completed the rout by dislodging it from the social and psychological worlds respectively. The individual human being is not, claims Althusser, the constituting subject which creates the world, society, history and the self. S/he does not even constitute knowledge of those worlds. Rather s/he is the helpless product of psycho-social processes beyond his/her control.

Althusser draws heavily upon the work of Lacan for his theory of ideology in general. Lacan reinterprets Freud's account of the oedipal drama, identifying its processes as conditions for the entry of the human child into language and society. In the course of this process, s/he also acquires a psycho-social identity, or self. The self is sexed, but otherwise undifferentiated, and is the subject of consciousness, experience, and practical activity. It is not, however, the unitary self of Cartesian philosophy and common sense which is constituted in ideology. The child acquires its identity through recognising itself in the idealised image of another. The other which mirrors the self is unlike the powerless, helpless and incoherent *'hommelette'* which is the pre-oedipal child, but appears to that child to be powerful, coherent and in command of the self and the world. The self misrecognises itself in this idealised image which it forms of itself in the mirror which is the idealised other. The 'I' of experience and consciousness is both necessary for social life, and at the same time based upon a necessary misconception.

The first mirror in which the self is defined is the idealised other which confronts the pre-oedipal child in the structure of the family. But other 'mirrors' are offered, throughout life. The self is nothing but the combined product of these imaginary reflections, and is as inconsistent as they are. Marxist cultural studies has drawn upon this imagery of the mirror in its discussion of film, literature and other cultural forms. In so far as they, too, offer seeming mirrors to the self, in which the self can (mis)recognise itself, social reality and its place within that reality, then cultural forms belong to the level of ideological practice within the social formation. In particular, it is realist forms which, it is held, play the mirror and so operate to produce the (ideological) subjects of experience and consciousness. Hence the anti-realist stance of this theory of cultural production.

It is because this misrecognition, which ideological production generates, is a real effect with real social functions that Althusser wants to refuse for ideology the label of 'false consciousness'.* Paul Hirst makes the point as follows:

> Ideology is not illusory . . . it is not falsity, because how can anything which has effects be false? It would be like saying that a black pudding or a steamroller is false. (Hirst, 1976, p16)

This is disingenuous, since black puddings and steamrollers are not propositions and therefore cannot be false. But ideologies, even those which are 'lived', can be expressed as propositions and therefore, unlike black puddings etc., can both be false and have effects. To assert the falsity of ideology is not to deny its effects. The concept of false consciousness in fact lurks close behind that of 'misrecognition'. It is, I would argue, not the recognition which it produces that marks ideology off from science, but the nature of that which is 'recognised'. Science too, as I have argued, depends upon recognition. It follows that no practice as such can be labelled ideological, unless it can be shown that the effect is to *mis*-represent the subject and his/her relationship to real conditions of existence. Unless we assume with Althusser and Lacan that all representation and all recognition is necessarily misrepresentation and misrecognition, then representation/recognition cannot serve as the identifying marks of ideological production.

What is new in Althusser's theory of ideology is not the denial of epistemological status to ideology (as Hirst claims). Althusser equivocates on this anyway, and frequently refers to theoretical and systematic bodies of thought as ideological. Nor does it lie in the proposition that ideological practices have real effects. Lukács and the other so-called marxist humanists of the twentieth century were guilty, if anything, of imputing too much rather than too little effect to ideology. Althusser's departure is rather his radical separation of science from ideology, so that they become quite different kinds of things with quite different social effects and functions, and his appropriation of the phenomena of consciousness, experience and action for the realm of ideology, their exclusion from knowledge production. For given that the 'I' of experi-

*The concept of 'false consciousness' is most closely associated with the work of Lukács. For a discussion of Lukács' theory of knowledge, ideology and false consciousness, see Chapter 4.

ence and consciousness is always misconceived for Althusser and Lacan, then if science is to be kept safe in the sterilised citadel of epistemological adequacy, it must avoid all contamination by the subject and its experience; hence his anti-empiricism. His theory of science must go beyond the realist critique of empiricism, and deny *any* role to experience and subjectivity in knowledge production. Conversely, if experience, action and subjectivity are phenomena of ideology, then a universalistic theory of ideology is required. For ideology could no more wither away than could experience, consciousness and the sense of self.

It is unquestionably the case — it is tautologous — that experience unaided by the practices of knowledge production cannot produce knowledge. Empiricist theories of knowledge which do not recognise the non-experiential elements of knowledge production are quite properly criticised. But it does not follow that experience has no place in knowledge production. It is possible, I would argue, to recognise the importance of the empirical in knowledge production without thereby falling into empiricism. Empiricism versus conventionalism offers the false choice of either experience or theory. Realism refuses the choice, and tries to develop a theory of knowledge in which each have their proper place, without displacing the other.

ii. *The Constituted Subject, Practical Activity and the Class Struggle*
It might be supposed that as Althusser defines knowledge production as a practice he is maligned by the suggestion that practical activity has no place in his theory of knowledge production. But the 'practices' which define knowledge production for Althusser are the specialised practices which have always gained recognition in the philosophy of science — theory construction, critical and methodological work, etc. It is important to remember that the theories in question are theories of the social formation. That is to say — in Althusser's own terms — theories of the various practices which constitute that formation, and the relationships which hold between them. The practical activities which are excluded from any place in knowledge production are *those practical activities which are to be explained.* Thus only the practical activities of 'theoretical practice' itself and not those of political practice, economic practice, etc., are held to be relevant to the construction of theories of those political, economic practices. To engage on a day-to-day basis *in* those practical activities accords the actor no special privileges when it comes to reconstructing those activities in knowledge. It is enough, I think, to state these implications to see how far they are from the union of theory and practice which has always been axiomatic for marxism. Mao's slogan that correct ideas come from revolutionary practice may be crude, but is closer to Marx's sociology of knowledge. Althusser, it is true, draws back from what he himself recognises to be theoreticism in *Lenin and Philosophy* and subsequent works. He attempts to rebuild

bridges between the class struggle and marxism as a theory of the social formation. However, in so doing he undermines much of his own theory of knowledge and ideology, in particular his theory of the constituted subject. For the concept of 'the class struggle' reintroduces a constitut*ing* subject, collective rather than individual, which is capable of informed intervention, in the hope of reasonably accurate anticipation of the effects which that intervention may produce. While Althusser theorises the constitut*ion* of the individual subject in ideology, he leaves no more room for a constitut*ing* collective, than for an individual, subject. Hirst again puts the point succinctly:

> The subject lives 'as if' it were a subject, and through the 'as if' it really does have a determinate effect. (Hirst, 1976, p13)

This will hardly do as the basis for 'the class struggle', which requires more than an 'as if' subject. A subject which *may* produce effects other than those intended is one thing, and inevitable when the reactions of others have to be anticipated, as well as a host of other intangibles. Predicting the results of actions is always difficult. But a subject which can in principle only produce effects it did not intend is quite another thing altogether, and hardly provides a stirring call to political engagement. For if the subject were capable of producing intended effects, it would after all be a real, constituting subject and not just an 'as if' constituted one.

For Marx, the subject of history is the class struggle, and the subjects of that struggle are social classes constituted by the social relations of production. It is true that the history they make is not always or perhaps ever identical to the history they intend to make:

> Men make their own history, but they do not make it just as they please; they do not make it under circumstances chosen by themselves . . . (Marx, 1962, p247)

But intentionality cannot be evacuated from the concept of the class struggle and the making of history; it is always a struggle to make history knowingly, to bring the circumstances of its making under the greatest possible degree of conscious control; to become full subjects of history.

iii. Individual and Class Subjects, and Sexed Identity

Marx, it is true, provides no theory of the constitution of the individual subject. It has been argued (Molina, 1977) that he nevertheless leaves space for such a theory. Yet at the very least any theory of the individual subject which purports to complement historical materialism must be broadly compatible with Marx's account of the class subject and its constitution within the structure of social relations. The theory of the subject which Althusser borrows from Lacan cannot be a candidate as it stands, for it contains no reference from start to finish to social class and the social relations of production. It is undifferentiated, identical for all human individuals of whatever class, in any society. The constituted individual human being that is the product of ideological practice is differentiated along lines of sex alone. It is because Lacan offers an explanation of sexed identity that his theory has interested marxist feminists. I do not have the space here, nor am I competent, to engage in a detailed discussion of Lacan's work. But it is clear that any attempt to construct an account of language, culture and sexed identity as ambitious as that of Lacan, requires an adequate theory of sexuality, male and female. This Freud failed to provide in respect of female sexuality, as he himself partly recognised. He wrote in 1926, '. . . the sexual life of adult women is a "dark continent" for psychology,' (Freud, 1977, p326) and is alleged to have remarked to Marie Bonaparte:

> The great question that has never been answered and which I have not yet been able to answer, despite my thirty years of research into the feminine soul, is 'What does a woman want?' (ibid.)

While he made several provisional answers to this question, none of them is finally satisfactory. Lacan's theory of sexuality recasts that of Freud, but remains in certain respects close to the original. He argues that language depends upon structuring differences, and that *the* privileged signifier whose presence/absence structures entry into language, culture and self-identity, is the phallus. Possession/non-possession of the phallus defines the sexes, and women are therefore defined in terms of a structuring absence or lack.

Several observations must be made here. In the first place, women no more 'lack' the phallus than men 'lack' the clitoris. Freud recognised the clitoris as in a sense the female organ which was equivalent to the male penis. Its existence was I suspect an embarrassment to his theory, and its importance had to be discounted by *ad hoc* means. It is, he claims, an inferior organ by virtue of its relatively small size and its inadequacy for purposes of penetration. Little girls, perceiving on sight of their brothers' superior member that they have been sadly short-changed, reject it in anger, and give up active clitoral masturbation in favour of feminine passivity centred on the vagina. Failure to achieve this transfer condemns them as immature. That this will hardly do has been the response of many commentators ever since Freud wrote his works on female sexuality. It assumes for one thing that size alone is the criterion that children use in assessing one another's sexual organs. Yet childhood imagery abounds in celebrating that which is small, secret, hidden away. More seriously, despite his acknowledgement of 'polymorphous perversity', he assumes that the aim of infantile sexuality is possession of the mother, and that full sexual possession requires penetration, an assumption which lesbians might find rather quaint. Lacan builds upon these inadequate foundations without serious challenge, rather compounding error upon error. Penis/clitoris are not opposites but contraries. Possession of one (usually) excludes possession of the other. But contraries can be transformed into oppositions using binary logic, as follows:

Penis/clitoris
Clitoris = lack of penis
Penis/lack of penis (Elimination of clitoris)

What Lacan does is to conflate two oppositions (penis/lack of penis, and clitoris/lack of clitoris) into a single opposition. As a result, the very real clitoris is excised, and replaced by an 'absence' or 'lack'. The real structuring absence of female sexuality, language and culture is not the penis (in its symbolic form as the phallus) but the clitoris. In societies which practice clitoridectomy it is literally absent. In ours, the castration is merely symbolic. We just don't talk about it, and we exercise an effective taboo on masturbation for young girls where their brothers are now allowed that privilege by enlightened liberal parents. Sex education in schools rarely touches on female sexual pleasure, and the predominant phallocentric sexual practices of our culture minimise that pleasure.

Curiously, Lacan's theory of language reproduces this structuring absence of our language and culture, instead of theorising it. For this reason alone, quite apart from any other inadequacies it may have, Lacan's theory cannot play the part which marxist feminism requires of it.

In addition to this fundamental problem, Lacanian theory of sexed identity is incompatible with marxism, although this need not trouble Lacan himself, nor any of his followers who do not claim to be marxists. But an account of sexed identity which locates the constitution of women so massively in the first few years of life cannot yield any independent role to the social relations of production. While this focus has brought the family to the centre of analysis, a place which it has never had within marxist theory, yet it loses sight of the place of women in production. Production and the social relations of production are also structured along lines of sex, and this structuring cannot be entirely explained in terms of the sexual division of labour within the family. We must not allow marxism to lose sight of the family, but a 'marxist' theory of the family must be compatible with the marxist theory of production. Clearly some mutual accommodation and modification may be necessary. But the family, from a marxist point of view, is not best characterised as a separate level of the social formation which *then* comes into articulation with other levels. The individual is not constituted as a social subject within a timeless and classless patriarchal order, nor does that individual, already sexed through his/her induction into the partiarchal order of the family, *then* acquire class identity upon entry to the labour market and economic production. The antagonistic relations between labour and capital are already present within the familial forms of capitalism. Within the family the major differences are those of sex and generation. In finding his/her place within the family these identities are learnt by the child. But the family itself has a class identity which all its members share, and which is acquired, along with sexed identity, by new recruits. It is this class differential *between* families which allows for the intrusion of antagonistic class relations into the very process of the constitution of the subject in the first place. Yet it is entirely ignored in Lacan's theory. We learn nothing about an identification of self based on similarity rather than difference, on shared class membership. If Marx is blind to sex, Lacan is equally blind to class. Yet Althusser has adapted Lacan's work to his purpose quite uncritically. When we speak of 'the family', 'the state', 'ideology', etc. this is more usefully interpreted as the *capitalist* family, state and ideology; as particular familial, state and ideological *forms* which these institutions take in different social formations. The fact that these relations are antagonistic means that the class struggle does not have to be smuggled into the analysis under cover of more fundamental and timeless antagonisms of patriarchy. It is present from the beginning in its own right. This covering of class and political struggles by the struggles of patriarchy can be seen in recent film analysis: Bellour's analysis of *North by Northwest* (Bellour, 1975); the *Cahiers* editorial analysis of *Young Mr Lincoln* (Cahiers, 1970). It is made quite explicit in an article by Colin MacCabe:

> What would mark such a cinema and indeed any cinema of subversion would be . . . the fact that it would be ill at ease in the class struggle, always concerned with an area of contradiction beyond the necessity of the present revolution — *the ineliminable contradictions of the sexes, the eternal struggle between Desire and Law,* between articulation and position. (MacCabe, 1974, p21) (my emphasis)

These kinds of interpretation are the inevitable outcome of an a-political, a-historical theory of the constitution of the subject and its entry into language and culture. Political and social relations can only be seen as avatars, or derivations, of the more fundamental conflicts of patriarchy and the primary process. The relations of labour/capital are in danger of being reduced to the revolt of the son against the Father, a reductionism no more acceptable than the economism which Althusser and his followers were at such pains to avoid.

Towards a (Narrower) Theory of Ideology

In this chapter I will begin by drawing out the implications of the previous two for a marxist theory of ideology, knowledge and experience. The first such implication which must be drawn is that recent developments in the theory of ideology have stretched that concept to the point of uselessness. If it is to be a working concept within marxism, then it must be returned to more precise limits. One task of this chapter is to propose such limits.

I. IDEOLOGY, KNOWLEDGE, AND THE HUMAN SUBJECT

One consequence of the development of a more restricted concept of ideology would be its withdrawal from some of the arenas it has recently been extended to occupy: in particular, from its place in theories of the constitution of the individual subject of experience and consciousness. I believe that the benefits of such a withdrawal would be twofold. It adds nothing to our understanding of the process of the induction of the human infant into society, language and culture to label that process 'ideological', particularly when the concept continues to be applied to other phenomena which are prima facie very different. Secondly, the similarities and real connections which may be found to obtain between prima facie different phenomena may be the more readily detected and explained if those phenomena are not prematurely identified as 'the same'.

If condensation and displacement are central processes in the work of the unconscious, and if these are similar to certain common devices of literature, then this is an interesting fact whose implications should be explored and which may indicate that there is a connection between the two. But the science of cybernetics frequently detects formal similarities between quite different phenomena. For instance, the spread of disease has commonly been compared to the pattern of the diffusion of innovations. Formal models of the spread of new technologies are identical to formal models of the spread of disease, yet the causes of each are very different. To use language as a source of models of the processes of the unconscious is one thing and quite legitimate. All disciplines borrow from others in this manner. It is another matter to conflate the two. The unconscious may be structured like a language, but this is insufficient to support the assumption that the unconscious is a linguistic phenomenon, or that language emanates from the unconscious.

One consequence of the premature conflation of the two should be noted. It is the languages of art and of common sense that are identified with the processes of the unconscious and with ideological production, while the languages of science are excepted, and placed behind a *cordon sanitaire*. The univocal language of science is alone taken at its own self-valuation, where all others are subject to close ideological interrogation. (As a matter of fact, a similar interrogation of scientific 'discourse' might prove extremely interesting. Despite the attempt to remove the subject from knowledge production, science, too, 'interpellates a subject' in its discourse. That subject is impersonal, objective, dispassionate — and male. In positing 'theoretical practice' as a practice without a subject, Althusser is paradoxically reproducing in his theory the self-image held in positivist/scientific discourse.) By definitional fiat, a close relationship is established between art, ideology and the unconscious, while the process of knowledge production is, by definition, separated by an uncrossable divide from all three.

Although I believe that the concept of ideology is misplaced here, I would not deny that under cover of that misplaced concept, questions have been raised and work has been produced which is of importance and interest. Marxism requires a theory of the subject, of the process whereby the human infant acquires a social, sexed identity, if it is to hope to make inroads into such areas as sex and gender patterning, the family, etc., with greater success than heretofore. I also believe that Lacan and Althusser are correct in turning to Freud as the recourse of first resort in this quest. The attempt to marry Freud and Marx has had, however, a long and not too encouraging history. If feminism is also to be thrown into the reckoning, then it is evident that what has to be undertaken is a fundamental rethinking and reworking of all three, and not just the filling out of the 'gaps' in marxism. As it stands, Freud's theory is, I believe, incompatible with both marxism and feminism. And Lacan's reworking of Freud, for reasons given in the last chapter, does not at present provide the basis for the reconstruction and reconciliation of the three.

It is beyond the scope of this work to adumbrate a marxist theory of sexed and classed individual identity. But the second area in which a strategic withdrawal of the pretensions of the theory of ideology may be required, that of cultural production, is one of central concern here. Again, while ideology and cultural production are certainly intimately connected, there is little to be gained from their premature identification. If ideology can be specified more narrowly, less inclusively, then the degree of closeness/distance between ideology and given instances of cultural production can be gauged. We are not entitled to assume that cultural production *per se* is also and at the same time the production of ideology, even where that cultural production takes the form of capitalist commodity production. I shall try to establish this point in the second half of this chapter, where the effects of the penetration of capital into cultural production will be explored.

2. KNOWLEDGE AND EXPERIENCE

In Chapter 2 I argued that Althusser's appropriation of the categories of experience and practical activity for ideology must be refused. Experience and practical activity are as central to the production of knowledge as of ideology. Marx's sociology of knowledge assumes that the kinds of practical activities in which people are engaged are in important part a function of the position which they occupy within the structure of social relations, and that this in turn limits and colours the subject's experience of self and the world. The way in which the self and the world are experienced will in turn structure the kinds of explanations which will be sought and found plausible with regard to that world.

In other words, marxism relates theory to the world not via the distanced, disinterested and 'objective' contemplation of the positivist account (the idea that marxist 'discourse' places the subject differently to positivism) but by practical, interested activity in and on the world, with a view to changing it. It is this link between knowledge and human interest which it shares with ideology and which is lost when they are defined as radically different kinds of practice.

In Chapter 1 I briefly indicated the role which the concept of commodity fetishism has in the construction of a marxist theory of ideology. The form which social relations take under capitalism is that of a relationship between things, through the exchange of commodities. This peculiar form of the social relations of capitalism generates certain typical experiences which will vary according to the position which the subject occupies (and *pace* Althusser and Lacan, the manner of their constitution as subjects, by class and sex). It is these common experiences which permit *both* the explanatory theories of science *and* those of theoretical ideology to draw upon an answering recognition which determines their acceptance and use, so that those theories 'come into their own in action' as Walter Benjamin put it. The 'truths' which everyone (mis)recognises in the ideological theories of political economy depend upon 'what everyone knows' through experience. These truths are the truths of the market place: '. . . a very Eden of the innate rights of man. There alone rule Freedom, Equality, Property and Bentham.' (Marx, 1970, p176) But political economy depends equally upon the denial or suppression of other experiences — those of production, when the point of view of the proletariat is adopted. The fact that the nature and basis of production is systematically obscured in political economy does not mean that production and the social relations of production are 'lived' only in the terms offered by political economy. Terms which have no place in that discipline may nevertheless inform the way in which the direct producer orders his/her experience of that production, and find partial and contradictory expression in common sense and popular lore. Working-class organisation and political struggle sharpen these concepts and bring them to the fore, where they may be developed and transformed in systematic theories such as those of marxism. But unless these theories can speak to the experiences which political economy necessarily distorts, ignores or denies, unless they can evoke 'recognition' on the basis of experience, then its truths might as well be falsities, for they will fail to meet the acid test of marxist knowledge, the test of practical, political activity.

A fundamental premiss then of any marxist theory of ideology must be that there are key areas of experience and practical activity which are suppressed, denied or distorted within the dominant ideology. While their suppression makes it difficult to give them a name, and to understand their significance, they are essential to knowledge production and to the critique of ideology. This was the point of the example in the last chapter of female sexuality. The development of a feminist 'discourse' on sexuality depends on the recovery of suppressed experience, and not simply upon 'theoretical practice'. It depends on an appeal to experiences which prevailing theories and practices deny. The *Hite Report*, empiricist as it is, is nevertheless eloquent testimony to the existence of levels of experience outside of the prevailing ideological order. (Hite, 1977) A 'theoretical practice', which places itself beyond experience, also places itself out of touch with any reality except the reality of its own 'discourse', and out of touch with politics.

Marx's theory of capitalism is not just a 'discourse' which exists alongside the opposed and incommensurable discourse of political economy. Rather it is a rival theory of the same object, capitalism. It rests its claim upon its ability to explain not only its own objects but those of political economy also. The experiences on which political economy draws for its validating 'recognition' are those of the market place. In explaining the nature of capitalist production, Marx also explains market relations, and the reasons why they have the appearances which they do. In this explanation, it is true, Marx redescribes these market relations in terms which are alien to political economy. But this kind of redescription is endemic in all explanatory theories. Incommensurability of description does not preclude overlap or even identity of objects described. The object of reference of scientific theories belongs to the world and not to theory.

I have referred here to political economy as ideological without so far giving any grounds for so doing. What is it that constitutes a body of ideas as ideological rather than scientific? Political economy makes precisely the same claim to validity as does marxism. How are such claims to be assessed? In Chapter 2 I examined the various criteria offered by Althusser to demarcate science from ideology, namely: (a) counter-intuitiveness v 'obviousness'; (b) closure v openness; and (c) the extra-theoretical v theoretical determination of problems. I argued that none of these criteria, separately or together, is adequate to that task of demarcation, and that formal criteria alone were unlikely to prove sufficient. In what follows I do not wish to deny that ideology is constituted in and by practice, and that ideological production is institutionalised. But in whatever form it appears, ideology may always be expressed in terms of a body of ideas, and I wish to argue that it is certain substantive properties of these ideas which allow us to refer both to them, and to the institutions and practices in which they are produced, as ideological.

What theoretical ideologies share with 'the lived' is not some peculiar mode of meaning production common to both — on the contrary, they produce their meanings according to quite different rules — but the end product, the meanings which they share. Whether or not certain meanings are ideological depends on the meaning produced, and not on the manner of its production. Ideologies are produced in quite different manners in the different practices of cultural production.

(a) The concept of ideology carries an irreducible critical dimension. Beliefs or bodies of ideas which are ideological are in some sense inadequate, partial or distorted. This alone is not, of course, enough to identify ideologies. The history of science is in large part a history of error.

(b) Therefore to this first criterion must be added a second, that the inadequacies of ideology in terms of the claim to knowledge are socially motivated in relation to the class struggle. The close identification of ideology with class interest since the introduction of the concept is significant and should not be lost. But again, this second criterion on its own would not serve to identify ideologies. For there are bona fide bodies of knowledge which are developed and institutionalised in such a way that they serve the interest of domination. Any dominant class will, if and to the extent that it controls the means of knowledge production, attempt to ensure that that knowledge is produced and disseminated in a manner which serves its class interests, and that the kinds of knowledge produced will serve the same function. Ideology, then, may be defined as the production and dissemination of erroneous beliefs whose inadequacies are socially motivated. This definition recognises two other categories: erroneous beliefs which are not so motivated, and valid beliefs which are, but places them both outside the category of ideology.

(c) It follows that to speak of ideas as ideological is always to make some claims about their effects as well as about their validity. They are mobilisations within the class struggle, and can only be mobilised if they produce particular effects. Ideology, ideas in general, are developed in and through practical activity. With the division of labour they may, however, become relatively detached from their point of origin. They may be subject to elaboration and systematisation by specialists in the intellectual division of labour, within the institutions of the superstructure. Not all ideas are equally bound up, on a day-to-day basis, in the class struggle. As they become relatively detached from their source, they may appear, like Gramsci's 'traditional intellectuals', to be free-floating and autonomous. But their autonomy is relative to their ineffectiveness, and not as with Althusser's concept to their effectiveness. Theology, for instance, has its own history, significantly articulated with the history of the class struggle only at certain key moments. We are not compelled to engage in a search for the 'real' economic motivations behind every theological dispute in the manner which evokes the label of 'vulgar marxism'. Yet neither can such disputes be dismissed as of scholastic interest alone. For they provide the source of an 'ideological reserve army' which may be drawn into active service as and when required. This 'mobilisation effect' is of critical importance in ideological struggle. It is also the reason why Brecht was right to insist on tolerance for the avant-garde — for new intellectual and artistic experiments which seem on the face of it to be far removed from any political relevance. It goes without saying, however, that bourgeois ideology has its own avant-garde. Novelty is not the monopoly of 'progressive' forces in society, and novelty alone, even the revolutionary overthrow of existing forms and conventions, does not guarantee political credentials. How and whether political mobilisation of cultural innovations will take place depends in part upon the social origins of those developments.

For example, Christianity had great potential for political mobilisation in radical millennial movements in the middle ages because of its origins as a 'religion of the oppressed'. Elements of its subversive radicalism survived its transformation into a respectable Imperial religion, and were kept alive in popular traditions which the Church could not altogether contain. It follows that we must pose, in addition to the more usual questions of the ideological *roots* of a given cultural development, that of its *potential* for political mobilisation. The ability of bourgeois ideology to recuperate anything and everything, including the most apparently radical images and ideas has often been noticed and bewailed. But recuperation cuts two ways. Just as traditional intellectuals may be mobilised — *must* be, according to Gramsci — so traditional ideas and images may be radicalised when uprooted, and placed in contexts very different from those which produced them. The devil should not always be left with the best tunes.

The development of neat criteria for the demarcation of science and ideology is one thing, and difficult enough. It is quite another again to apply these criteria in individual cases. Some useful guidelines may be drawn:

(a) It is unlikely that any body of ideas or theory will fall unequivocally into one or another category. This is particularly so in the social sciences, where knowledge and interest are so closely linked.

(b) To establish that a given body of ideas or theory serves class interests is always insufficient to justify the label of ideology. It is always necessary *first* to apply epistemological criteria to evaluate the work. Only when the ideas in question have had their inadequacy to their object amply demonstrated, and when the respects in which they are inadequate are also shown to touch upon class interest in a systematic way, is the critique of ideology completed. The common practice of discrediting ideas by reference to their social origin is not what is meant by this critique. Questions of validity are always also involved. We can learn a good deal here from Marx's own practice. His procedure is first of all to establish by theoretical analysis, argument and evidence, an account of whatever is in contention. He then goes on to show precisely in which respects a rival theory falls short of explanatory power. Only then does he attempt to relate those specific errors to class alignments and the class struggle. An example of this method is to be found in Volume III of *Capital* where he considers the evidence given by bankers in the *Report of the Committee on Bank Acts of 1857*. He assesses this evidence in terms of its internal inconsistencies, and its theoretical and empirical inadequacies. He then goes on to argue that these views are to be expected from bankers at this time, because of the form which social relations take in general under capitalism, and because of the particular position of bankers within that structure of social relations and the interests which that position generates. His argument is, in effect: 'this is indeed how money and banking *would appear* to people so situated, and these are the categories which they *would require* in their day-to-day conduct of their business activities.' (Marx, 1970) This procedure is exemplary, but is seldom followed by people wishing to expose the ideological underpinnings of their opponents' thought.

(c) It is not necessary, in order to establish the bona fides of any body of theory, that it should be able to claim 'objectivity' in the sense of having no axe to grind, no relationship to the class struggle. Marxism does not have to be detached from the point of view of the proletariat with which it has been traditionally associated. On the contrary, to do so is to cut the ground from beneath it.

i. *The Social Relations of Production*

In Althusserian and post-Althusserian discussions of ideology, the attempt has been made to substitute for the concept of 'reflection' that of ideological *production*. This concept of ideological production has the consequence of drawing attention to the fact that ideology is the product of distinct processes which must be analysed. But the Althusserian concept of production is too narrow, in that it does not include *the* key concept of Marx's theory of production, the *social relations of production*. In this section I want to see what purchase the concept of 'ideological production' has on the analysis of cultural production when the concept of social relations of production is restored. In what follows I will be looking at some of the consequences which follow from the penetration of capital into the production of commodities which are bearers of ideology.

Althusser uses the concept of production almost interchangeably with that of practice. As stated in Chapter 2, he defines practice in general as:

> . . . any process of *transformation* of a determinate given raw material into a determinate *product*, a transformation effected by a determinate human labour, using determinate means (of 'production'). In any practice thus conceived, the *determinant* moment (or element) is neither the raw material nor the product, but the practice in the narrow sense: the moment of the *labour of transformation* itself . . . (Althusser, 1977a, p166)

The social relations of production are absent from this definition, implying presumably that production can be defined independently of the social relations within which it occurs. Ideology is a practice, and as such, its material base is not some other practice which it reflects, but its own material productive processes, especially its own particular 'labour of transformation' or work process. Looked at in relation to cultural production in the case of such artefacts as film or literature, the process of transformation in question is, by definition, that of ideological production in general; the process of transforming/confirming individuals as subjects by 'interpellating' them in the text as readers, viewers, etc. The question which has to be addressed to the text, then, is not 'how does it reflect social reality?' but 'by what means is the ideological effect of the interpellation of the subject achieved through the processes whereby meaning is constructed in the text?' The resulting analysis is overwhelmingly concentrated upon the text, due to the absence of interest in the social relations of (textual) production, and is at times remarkably close to quite orthodox methods of literary textual analysis. Since the subject who is the reader of the text is constructed by the text, there is no need to look beyond the text to actual readers or viewers and the ways in which they have been affected by their reading of the text. The effect is read off from the text itself, by analysing the manner in which it constructs the social subjects who consume it and who are confirmed as subjects by and through this consumption.

This narrow textualism is complemented in the case of film by an additional if contrary approach via 'the apparatus' of film consumption. Jean-Louis Baudry has written an influential piece which claims that it is the very structure of the viewing situation which produces the ideological effect — the relationship between screen, image, projector and viewer. (Baudry, 1976) With this approach even textual analysis becomes redundant, for whatever the ostensible subject of the film, whatever its 'signifying practice', the ideological effect will be the same so long as the structure of the viewing situation remains the same. The inadequacy of both of these approaches stems from the metaphorical concept of production, in the absence of 'social relations of production'. Without this category production is narrowed down to its own technology, the technology of production or, in the case of Baudry, consumption. In the first case it becomes identical with what Marx termed 'the labour process'. Once the missing term is supplied the limitations of both textualism and the approach through the viewing apparatus become clear, for the social relations of production cannot be read off from the text, nor from the mode of its consumption. Yet they have consequences of an important kind for ideological production.

Before proceeding it is necessary to be more precise about the concept of 'ideological production'. Ideology as defined in the first part of this chapter is a second order concept. We cannot assume that any given text is a text of ideological production, in any given genre or type of product. Indeed there are, I would argue, very few social institutions which can be identified as specifically ideological. Rather there are a number of institutions which produce different kinds of products or initiate different kinds of activity, which are all in their different ways bearers of ideology. Orwell's Ministry of Truth was quite explicitly and consciously engaged in the production of propaganda and ideology, and for that reason it is not a terribly good model for ideological production under capitalism. The various legal, political, religious and cultural institutions produce laws, legal practices, religious ideas and rituals, literary texts, films, etc., each of which may stand in a different relationship to both contemporary science and the dominant ideology, a relationship which may moreover vary historically. We are not able to assume that a given work or practice produces the dominant ideology, just as we are unable by virtue of its formal properties, point of origin or manner of production, to assume that a given piece of theoretical work is ideological. We certainly cannot make the assumption that art is *per se* ideology. Particular works must first be analysed in terms of the ideas which inform them, the beliefs which they produce and perpetuate, the effects they have. It should also be noted here that if the concept of ideology is restricted to the realm of ideas, it follows that only to the extent that art rests upon ideas will the concept of ideology be applicable to it. In so far as there are other dimensions of art besides the cognitive, such as the emotive, evaluative and aesthetic, then further concepts will be required for its sociological analysis.

Cultural production is not then the same thing as ideological production. It can, however, be confidently assumed that the artefacts of cultural production will be important *bearers* of ideology, will not be neutral *vis-à-vis* the class struggle. But in the first instance we are dealing with the production of films, literature, television programmes, etc., and with ideology only in so far as analysis reveals them as such.

The concept of ideology has, I have argued, a certain functionalist connotation, through the notion of 'the ideological effect' — the relationship of ideology to class struggle. The ideological effect is an effect produced upon individuals and groups by the product which bears that ideology, which serves to support the interests of the dominant class or the needs of capitalism. It is produced only when those cultural artefacts which are the bearers of 'the ideological effect' are read, watched, listened to, by those individuals and groups. Althusser identifies several different arenas of ideological practice, of which the most important are the school, the family, the Church and the media. It may be seen at once why the concept of 'the social relations of production' is so crucial. For different institutions operate within significantly different social relations, and some of them have changed during the course of the history of capitalism. They may be distinguished initially, and for our purposes, into those which have been heavily penetrated by capital and those which have not. Clearly some areas of ideological production are more amenable to penetration than others. It is cultural production which has been most heavily penetrated, and again there are differences within and between different types of cultural production. For instance, some arts receive state support through such bodies as the Arts Council, British Film Institute and Regional Arts Associations, while television is organised through public corporations. Some require collective forms of production and work processes, others are individualistic, etc.

ii. Cultural Production and the Commodity Form

With the penetration of capital into cultural production, the product is transformed into a commodity. As such, cultural production shares features with *all* capitalist commodity production, and the most appropriate starting point for a marxist analysis of cultural production might be Marx's own categories for the analysis of capitalist commodity production. These are *use-value, value, exchange-value, surplus-value,* and *commodity fetishism.* Commodities have a double existence, as repositories of use-value and of value. Use-value, the utility or usefulness of a commodity to its consumer, depends on the ability of the commodity to satisfy some human want. Marx's concept of want is not limited to material needs. He says that wants 'may spring from the stomach or from the fancy'. In most cases when the commodity is used, it is also used *up*. The use-value of a commodity is realised only when it is consumed, or used.

The *value* of a commodity depends not on its usefulness, but on the amount of socially necessary labour time which has been expended in its production. The value which a commodity has is realised only when the commodity is exchanged. The rate at which one commodity exchanges for another on the market is its *exchange-value*. This also depends on the amount of socially necessary labour time which each commodity embodies. Money is that commodity which is used as a measure of value and means of exchange.

Cultural artefacts are commodities of a peculiar kind, in part precisely because they satisfy wants which spring from the fancy not the stomach, while Marx's own analysis was based on the latter kind of want satisfaction. They are unlike material wants, in that the commodities which satisfy them are not always used up when they are used to satisfy that want. Commodities which satisfy material wants vary, it is true, in the extent to which their use involves consumption, or using up. Houses last much longer than motor cars, which in turn are used up on a much longer time scale than, say, food. But in each case there is some relationship between the amount of use and the commodities wearing out. Cultural artefacts vary in the extent to which their usefulness in satisfying wants which 'spring from the fancy' is bound up with physical form. Some artefacts such as paintings or sculptures wear out over a very long time, and there is no direct connection between their use and their being used up. The Mona Lisa does not wear out more quickly when viewed by a hundred people rather than one person in the course of a day. Its physical deterioration depends on the conditions under which it is exhibited rather than the number of viewers. Other cultural forms are less closely tied to particular physical forms. For instance, a poem or a song can be learned and repeated, and cannot be used up no matter how often it is used to satisfy some want. The more frequently it is used, the greater its power of survival. The disc on which the song is recorded is the commodity form in this case, but want satisfaction may be independent of this form. The song can be transferred onto a tape, and serve equally well.

These differences between commodities of different kinds were not analysed by Marx, nor systematically by any subsequent marxists. Yet they have consequences for the development of the commodity form in cultural production. Some of these consequences may be seen in the difficulties which capitalism has in placing essential marks of ownership upon such commodities, through copyright and its protection, difficulties which are compounded by certain forms of mechanical reproduction, as witness recent attempts to control illicit taping of records. The problem stems ultimately from the lack of intrinsic connection between the usefulness to the consumer of a particular type of cultural artefact, and the physical form of commodity under which it is sold. This example indicates the need for an investigation of the effects of the transformation of cultural products into commodities, the difficulty of pinning down cultural product to commodity form.

iii. Cultural Production and Left Pessimism

The use-value of a commodity cannot be known in advance of investigation of actual use of that commodity. Marx has very little to say about the use-value of commodities, with the exception of the commodity labour-power. The reason for Marx's neglect is capitalism's own indifference. Capitalist commodity production is *per se* interested only in the production of *surplus-value*. The extent to which the production and sale of cultural products as commodities can generate surplus-value depends on their value-form and not their use-value. Their value-form depends on the labour they contain, not the use to which they are put. Of course commodities must also be repositories of use-value, otherwise they would not sell. The capitalist producer is keenly interested in the proliferation of wants which will lead consumers to seek out the commodities sold to satisfy those wants.

The focus on the transformation of cultural production into capitalist commodity production is not new, but has usually been associated with 'left pessimism' in the history of marxism, for instance that of the Frankfurt School. Cultural production, from a left pessimist point of view, is the production of shoddy goods, once culture is transformed into commodities. It is argued that the constraints of reaching the largest possible market places a premium on blandness, inoffensiveness, the lowest common denominator of public taste.* Left pessimism cannot cull much support for this view from the writings of Marx, however. As we have seen, the capitalist producer of commodities must be keenly interested in the proliferation of wants, and Marx saw this as the chief justification of capitalism historically. He wrote of:

> . . . the search for means to spur workers on to consumption to give [the] wares new charms, to inspire them with new needs by constant chatter, etc. It is precisely this side of the relation of capital to labour which is an essential civilising moment, and on which the historical justification, but also the contemporary power of capital rests. (Marx, 1973, p287)

*The work of P. Golding and G. Murdoch offers a contemporary example of this type of argument. See 'For a Political Economy of Mass Communication', *Socialist Register*, R. Milliband and J. Saville (eds.), Merlin Press, London 1973.

Where Marx, in this decidedly positive evaluation of capitalism, sees the civilising effects of the proliferation of wants, left pessimism sees only a loss of standards, a cultural down-grading process. There is no suggestion to be found in Marx's writings that commodities are, as such, second-rate goods, nor that the wants which they satisfy are not 'real' wants. For Marx there is no such category, essential to left pessimism, as 'false needs'.

While it is true that not all use-values can take the form of a commodity and that the development of the commodity form transforms use-values, it cannot be assumed that this automatically involves loss of quality. The cult of the hand-made craft product assumes that standardisation means loss. Good home-cooked meals are contrasted with degenerate tv dinners. Yet even in catering, standardisation may mean the raising of standards in general, in some respects. Traditional peasant cooking and Elizabeth David reconstructions thereof for middle-class dinner parties are worlds apart, and both in turn differ from Trust Houses Forte and tv dinners. But Elizabeth David cookery shares with the latter that it is a consequence of the development of the commodity form, and is misrepresented as a simple refusal of that form, a harking back to earlier, pre-capitalist use-values.

iv. Some Contradictions of Capitalist Penetration of Cultural Production
The key to capitalist commodity production lay, for Marx, in the contradiction between the use-value and the value of the commodity labour-power. Labour-power is that commodity which has, as its use-value for its purchaser, the ability to create value. So long as that labour-power is used to produce greater value than the exchange-value (the wage) which was paid for it, then the result will be the production for its capitalist purchaser of *surplus value*. Using this key example, we may infer that the use-value of a commodity may be in contradiction with its value. This potential contradiction can be seen in Marx's analysis of the capitalist system of production as a whole. Its operation requires that different commodities be produced in a certain proportion to each other and in relation to social necessity. In Volume II of *Capital*, (Marx, 1970) he discusses this necessary proportion between what he terms 'Departments I and II' of production — production for individual consumption, and for 'productive consumption' (producer goods) respectively. In his analysis Marx shows how it is possible for this relationship between production in the two Departments to be in equilibrium. Ernest Mandel shows that this is a special case which cannot be assumed always to obtain. (Mandel, 1972) Capitalist production between the two Departments may be in disequilibrium, and the theory of combined and unequal development suggests that this greater or lesser disequilibrium must be the norm. In other words there is no inbuilt mechanism to ensure that production overall is as much as

and no more than is socially necessary, and in the required proportions.

'Social necessity' is a problematic concept in *Capital*. But we may assume that capitalism itself generates certain requirements for its own maintenance and well-being, some of which operate at the level of individuals, and others at the level of the social collectivity. For instance, there is a need for efficient systems of transport for the circulation of commodities which is essential to the capitalist commodity form. The very concept of ideology points to another area of the requirements of capitalism.

Some of these diverse needs of capitalism are met within institutions which are not, or not fully, penetrated by capital. They are needs which are not, or cannot be, met by the purchase and sale of commodities. Much ideological production takes place in schools, homes, the church, etc., and in all of these the production of 'the ideological effect' does not depend on the consumption of a commodity. What must be raised here is the question of what happens when, with the penetration of capital, the production of 'the ideological effect' does become dependent upon the consumption by individuals and groups, of commodities? The commodities in question — films, books, television programmes, etc. — have different use-values for the individuals who use and purchase them than they have for the capitalists who produce and sell them, and in turn, for capitalism as a whole. We may assume that people do not purchase these cultural artefacts *in order* to expose themselves to bourgeois ideology, the 'ideological effect', but to satisfy a variety of different wants which can only be guessed at in the absence of analysis and investigation. There is no guarantee that the use-value of the cultural object for its purchaser will even be compatible with its utility to capitalism as bourgeois ideology, and therefore no guarantee that it will in fact secure 'the ideological effect'. For example, the utility of a television programme for a producer who buys advertising time is the ability of that programme to enhance the sale of the advertised product, by giving the producer access to the audience which is watching the programme. But the viewer will be watching that programme for its entertainment value and there is some evidence that these two interests may conflict. A programme which is a best seller and which its audience rates very highly on entertainment value may actually be less effective as a vehicle for impressing advertised products and increasing their sales than a less entertaining programme.

This particular example illustrates conflicts which may occur between the use-value of a commodity and its utility for particular capitals. But this conflict may also obtain between the use-value in question and the interests of capitalism in general. Here the conflict may be compounded by the divergence of interest between particular capitals and capitalism as a whole. Particular capitals invested in the entertainment industry have an interest in maximising profits through maximising the popularity and therefore the sale of entertainment. They have only a common class interest in securing the ideological needs of capitalism. This collective class interest may cut across the interest in the search for surplus value. If surplus value can be extracted from the production of cultural commodities which challenge, or even subvert, the dominant ideology, then all other things being equal it is in the interests of particular capitals to invest in the production of such commodities. Unless collective class restraints are exercised, the individual capitalists' pursuit of surplus value may lead to forms of cultural production which are against the interests of capitalism as a whole.

v. Use-Value, and the Pleasure of the Text

To examine this problem would require a shift from the point of view of capitalist commodity production, to that of consumption. Unfortunately we have no marxist theory of capitalist commodity consumption. The only school of marxist theory to address this question was the Frankfurt School, and for this reason it is a pity that its work has been dismissed as 'humanist' and 'historicist'. Despite its left pessimism, the Frankfurt School did raise important questions which other approaches have neglected.

Any marxist theory of consumption would have as its central category 'use-value', and would focus on 'the pleasure of the text'. It is true that Althusserian and Lacanian currents in cultural studies have turned to this important question of pleasure, but its meaning has been restricted to the narrow Freudian sense. Cultural products are articulated structures of feeling and sensibility which derive from collective, shared experience as well as from individual desires and pleasures. The pleasure of the text stems at least in part from collective utopias, social wish fulfilment and social aspirations, and these are not simply the sublimated expression of more basic sexual desires.

Whatever the locus and nature of the use-values of cultural products it remains certain that capitalist producers of those products must make and sell commodities which embody those use-values if they are to succeed in meeting the wants which they satisfy, and through doing so, generating surplus value. The producer must 'give the public what it wants' and what it wants does not necessarily sit square upon bourgeois ideology.

Of course, care must be taken to avoid the suggestion that those wants are the independent expression of the random and varied desires of the sovereign consumer. Wants are systematically, socially produced, and their production is not independent of the dominant mode of production of the society in which they occur. In part they are produced and elicited by the products themselves, so that at a single stroke, a want is created and a commodity produced to meet that want. The market for commodities is too important to capitalism to be left to consumer whim. Along with capitalist commodity production a whole host of means of stimulating and proliferating wants has been developed. Wants are not natural or eternal. Again this points to an area of investigation to which Marx himself gives few clues, and which has been neglected by marxism. The social production of wants under capitalism would constitute part of the absent marxist theory of capitalist consumption. But it may be hazarded that the production of wants is never fully under the control of the dominant class. Capitalism generates, by its very nature, a rich variety of wants. The satisfaction of many of these would not be desirable for capitalism, and some would be inimical to its interests, while others would be impossible to meet, difficult to control.

The paradoxical effects of the capitalist penetration of cultural production are a matter of conscious concern for certain groups outside the point of production itself — the ideologues and the professional guardians of public morality who swell the ranks of Gramsci's 'traditional intellectuals'. Every successive penetration of capital into cultural production has produced an outbreak of 'moral panic' in its wake. In the eighteenth century the rise of the novel produced widespread attack, allegations that it was morally pernicious in its effects upon weak-minded women and servants who were avid consumers of the new form. It was universally slammed, from pulpit to review. The same spectacle was repeated in our century over film in the thirties, and television in the fifties. The panic this time centred on equally weak-minded children and adolescents, for fear they would indulge in an orgy of imitative violence on exposure to the media. Effects studies have been the meat and drink of media specialists ever since. But there has been relatively little interest in the question of how and whether the 'anarchy of capitalist production' is offset in the interests of securing its ideological safety. The history of censorship should be looked at from this point of view. Censorship at least indicates which areas are considered sensitive or taboo. The increasing role of the state in the various areas of cultural production outside of a strict capitalist nexus would also repay study. For instance, the independent cinema may be independent of capitalist production, but is in turn dependent on the capitalist state, through the support of state-funded bodies such as the Arts Council. The approach to marxist cultural studies from the point of view of production has generated no greater interest in these questions than did reflection theories. When the concept of the social relations of production is reinstated, perhaps such questions will come into sharper focus.

Finally it is clear that a marxist perspective yields no *a priori* grounds for anticipating the results of ideological analysis of cultural production of the various media penetrated by capital, in the absence of any marxist theory of capitalist *consumption*. The theory of *production* too shows that cultural commodities are likely to express a wide variety of ideas, emotions, values and sensibilities, only some of which will be drawn from and articulated with the dominant ideology, and many of which will originate in class experience and class aspirations which are antithetical to capitalism. This type of analysis leaves room for different strategies of class struggle, based on workers within the heartland of the mass entertainment industry and not centring entirely on an avant-garde which has no mass appeal. We cannot read off the effects of cultural production from the manner of its production — from the fact that much of it takes the form of capitalist commodity production and is subject to the law of value. Nor, as we shall see in the next two chapters, can it be read off automatically from aesthetic form itself.

Realism and Marxist Aesthetics I

I. THE CONVENTIONS OF REALISM

If marxism is a realism, then it may seem unsurprising that marxist aesthetics has traditionally centred on this concept in theories of 'socialist' and 'critical' realism. The domination of marxism by an aesthetics of realism has never been complete, as the work of the Russian formalists and the Frankfurt School testifies. But it has received its most serious attack in recent marxist cultural studies, from a conventionalist perspective. I have challenged the conventionalist basis of that attack in the first two chapters of this work, and it might be expected that the defence of marxism as a realism might be followed by an attempt to reinstate marxist realist aesthetics. However, I want to argue that the connection between epistemological realism and realism in art is at best tenuous. The imperatives which follow for aesthetic theory and practice from marxist realism and materialism are by no means obvious.

Realism in art is almost as old as art itself. M. H. Abrams has traced the concept of mimesis in art from classical Greece to the present day. (Abrams, 1953) From the eighteenth century onwards there have been a number of movements in various arts — the novel, painting, film, etc. — which have styled themselves 'realist' and have seen themselves as making radical departures from existing practices under this title. Yet each of these 'realisms' has arisen in specific historical circumstances, and each takes its meaning as much from the practices to which it was opposed, as from practices common to all realisms. Realisms are plural, then, they nevertheless share more than an unsystematic 'family resemb-connotations which that term has subsequently acquired. It is the debased concept of evaluation of almost all contemporary popular criticism, and of common-sense thinking about cultural works, as may be seen from a random glance at film reviews in newspapers and popular magazines.

While the distinctiveness of different realisms must be acknowledged, then, they nevertheless share more than an unsystematic 'family resemblance'. When looked at historically, the shared assumptions and practices of these different realisms begin to emerge, as Raymond Williams has shown. Williams has provided us with by far the most careful sifting through of the connotations of realism as they developed historically, in order to enable us to identify the common core which they share. He locates this primarily in the realist claim that the business of art is first and foremost 'to show things as they really are'. But he comments:

> It does not end, but only begins a controversy in art and literature when it is said that the purpose is 'to show things as they really are'. (Williams, 1976, p218)

Moreover this claim for art is not unique to realism. It is common to all approaches which view art as a form of knowledge, and claim significant cognitive status for it. Realism involves, in addition to this claim, substantive theories about the nature of the reality which art purports to reveal, and these substantive theories are frequently drawn from one or another of the sciences. The difference between platonic and realist art does not lie in the latter's claim to reveal the real, but in radically opposed *accounts of* the real. A theory which looks at particular things as imperfect copies of ideal universal forms, as Platonism does,* will have no place for an art which is based on the close imitation of those particulars, for it would be third-hand art — an imitation of imitations. On these grounds Plato preferred to keep the poets in a low position in his ideal Republic. It follows that any particular realist movement, and the history of the succession of such movements, will have to be understood in terms of the changing theories of reality and changing methodologies on which these realisms were modelled. The aesthetic maxims and practices which they developed make sense only in this context. One reason for the pluralism of realisms is that different realist movements have drawn on one or another of the epistemologies discussed in Chapter 1, namely positivism and realism, and while these are two different theories of knowledge, artistic theories and practices based upon them have not always been kept distinct. Some realisms have been premised on positivist theories (for instance, nineteenth-century realist painting) while others have rested upon a critique of positivism (for instance Lukács's aesthetic writings), and on a distinction between the surface appearances of things and the underlying essences.

All realisms share, then, firstly the claim that the business of art is to show things as they really are, and secondly, some theory of the nature of the reality to be shown and the methods which must be used to show it. These theories and methods have often been modelled on the sciences. The task which realist movements then face is that of transcribing that

---

*Platonic theory had a revival in the nineteenth century with Romanticism. M. H. Abrams quotes Blake: 'No Man of Sense can think that an Imitation of the Objects of Nature is the Art of Painting ... facsimile representations of merely mortal and perishing substances ... Vision or Imagination is a Representation of what Eternally Exists, Really and Unchangeably', and is merely 'reflected in this Vegetable Glass of Nature'. (Abrams, 1953, p131)

which is to be known through art by using the rules and conventions, or 'signifying practices' which are held appropriate to that work. These rules and practices will vary with changes in the theoretical and methodological commitments of the realist movement in question. Because realist movements vary so much in their theories and methods, there has been a tendency to identify realism operationally, according to the actual rules and practices which movements which call themselves realist have adopted. But it would be a mistake, as Williams convincingly shows, to understand realism simply in terms of its shifting conventions:

> The terms 'realism' and 'naturalism' did not originally refer to conventions and technical methods in art, literature and drama, but to changed attitudes towards 'reality' itself, towards man and society, and towards the character of all relationships. (Williams, 1977, p30)

The conventions of realism will be shared among different realisms only to the extent that they share the same view of reality. If we look for what is common to them all, we will find that it is fairly minimal. Williams identifies the baseline rules of realism and naturalism in the following terms:

(a) Secularism: Cause-effect relationships should be presented in human and natural terms, without reference to supernatural forces.

(b) Contemporaneity: Action should be set in the present or recent past, not in the historical or mythical past.

(c) Social Inclusiveness: The action should be extended to include middle and lower classes.

Williams discusses the separation of naturalism from realism in the later nineteenth century, in terms of the different locus of the reality they wished to present, as well as different accounts of its dynamic. Naturalism interested itself in psychological, or 'inner' reality, and presented it in the context of the social and physical environment which formed the inner world. Realism focussed more upon the external social reality, which it saw as a human construct, the result of human interaction and therefore open to historical change as a result of human intervention. This led to stress upon the determining action of people upon their environment rather than their passive moulding by it. The differences between the conventions of naturalism and of realism in art can be partially traced to these different social and psychological theories.

Williams argues that while realism emerged as a bourgeois form against feudal and aristocratic conventions, it became in turn an instrument of social criticism in the hands of the working class. He declares, bluntly: 'the diagnosis of "realism" as a bourgeois form is cant.' (ibid., p30) He also insists that the relationship between realism and the formal and technical methods of presentation which have become established within any given art is a loose one. Realism as a critical instrument of working-class politics and sensibility must be flexible in its strategies, and must always consider questions of form and technique in relation to particular audiences as well as in relation to content.

Marxist materialism, as a particular variant of epistemological realism, rests, as we have seen, upon the belief that there are underlying forces and relationships which structure human interaction and determine the social dynamic and history. Because of the particular form which these social relationships take under capitalism, these underlying forces are not immediately visible to those who act in these social relationships. The fetishised form of the social relations of capitalism obscures those relations, but does so systematically, according to one's position within that structure of social relations, and according to the extent of the penetration of the dominant ideology. But if the real forces which structure the social world and history are not the actions and interactions of human beings, but the relationships between such things as labour and capital, then this immediately creates a problem. How can these causal relationships be shown through the use of realist conventions which are limited to the display of causes through individual human interaction? Secondly, how can the social world which characters in the novel and drama inhabit be shown, on the one hand realistically from the point of view of those characters and, on the other, in a manner such that the reader can penetrate beyond that point of view to the underlying dynamic of that world? Thirdly, if individual human beings are 'placed' within and by those underlying forces and relationships and the human intervention which changes them is essentially collective and political, then how can this be shown using conventions which are restricted to the representation of small-scale interaction between individuals?

These problems of reconciling marxism's particular theory of society, the individual and human action, with conventions which were developed in relationship to more humanistic concepts and theories, may possibly be resolved. There is no suggestion here that they are necessarily insurmountable, although it is equally clear that their resolution will entail modifications and adaptations of the theory and conventions of realism. The history of such concepts as 'critical realism' and 'socialist realism' is precisely the history of the attempt to forge conventions and theories of realism which are adapted to marxist theory and politics. The chief architect of this attempt was Georg Lukács.

i. The Theory of Knowledge

That Lukács was an epistemological realist is not open to doubt. He states this unequivocally. His essay entitled 'Art and Objective Truth' begins with the first premiss of realism, that there is an external world which exists independently of consciousness and knowledge of it. He goes on to claim that consciousness and knowledge are in some sense reflections of that external world. His second premiss is contained in the title of the essay, and is central to all realist theories of art. It is that art is a form of knowledge, different from science, but sharing the same goal, that of 'showing things as they really are'. As with science, art may be divided between those works which succeed in this task and those which do not. But if art, as a form of knowledge, is a reflection of the real, then Lukács is obliged to explain how it is that error and distortion are possible. Clearly we cannot be dealing with a mechanical process in which reality imprints itself upon the mind, and is transposed into art or science. Lukács has to develop a sociology of knowledge to explain the sources of both truth and error in reflections of the real.

Lukács's sociology of knowledge is found in his *History and Class Consciousness* (Lukács, 1968) and, despite his later retraction of that work as a condition of his political asylum in the Soviet Union, the positions which he developed there continue to inform much of his later work on aesthetics. Briefly, consciousness, according to Lukács, whether ideological or not, depends upon class position, and is a function of class activity and class interest. Historically, different social classes have been able to come more or less close to an understanding of the social world according to the manner which their class interests dictated. But the only class which occupies a position of privilege with respect to the production of knowledge of the social world as a whole is the proletariat. Only in the case of the proletariat does class interest require objective knowledge of the totality. Other classes are able to develop only partial knowledge, but for the proletariat, says Lukács, 'Ideology . . . is no banner to carry into battle . . . it is the objective and the weapon itself.' (ibid., p70) Unless the proletariat develops adequate and accurate knowledge of the social totality of capitalism, it will fail to monitor its political activities in such a way that its goal is achieved. The goal dictated by proletarian class interest is the overthrow of capitalism, the ushering in of socialism. Class interest converges with a broader, Hegelian teleology of history itself. For the proletariat is for Lukács a 'universal' class, capable of developing universal knowledge, because its interests, unlike those of other social classes in history, are not narrowly sectarian, and do not require the subordination or exploitation of any other class. In freeing itself, the proletariat frees mankind, and allows the realisation of 'man's species being'. The proletariat is a totalising class whose point of view coincides with objectivity and truth.

Lukács uses a similar argument to account for 'bourgeois' error. Like Marx, Lukács rated bourgeois thought and art very highly. But he thought that it was structurally inhibited from arriving at full knowledge of the social totality. He identified the limits of bourgeois thought in the limits beyond which it could not go without threatening its own social dominance as a class:

> . . . the objective limits of capitalist production become the limits of the class consciousness of the bourgeoisie . . . the veil drawn over the nature of bourgeois society is indispensable to the bourgeoisie itself. (ibid., pp64/6)

The bourgeoisie cannot afford a full understanding of capitalism because it would reveal its inevitable overthrow.

Lukács's theory explains only the objective possibility of the development of 'totalising' knowledge by the proletariat, but not the conditions of its production in actuality. He distinguished between this 'objective consciousness' (which he also termed 'imputed' or 'ascribed consciousness' and 'maximal possible consciousness') and the 'achieved' or 'psychological' consciousness of the actual historical proletariat at any given point in time. He recognised that there might be a considerable distance between the two. He drew upon Max Weber's ideal type methodology in developing these concepts. The 'imputed consciousness' of the proletariat is that consciousness which a fully rational actor would have, if in possession of all the relevant information about those things which touched upon his/her class situation and class interest. It is a 'rational reconstruction' of class consciousness, not an empirical description. It is a property of the class, and not of individuals, because no single individual can possibly be in the god-like position of perfect knowledge. It finds its nearest expression in the thought and action of the vanguard of the class, the Party.

It is still left for Lukács to explain how the situation/position of the proletariat within capitalism leads not merely to their having an interest in the development of this 'imputed consciousness' but to its actual historical development. The objective aspects of Lukács's theory are drawn from Marx's theory of commodity fetishism. Out of this theory, Lukács developed the concept central to his thought, that of 'reification'. Social relations are reified when, as under capitalism, they have the form of a relationship between things. The social world is changed and reconstructed throughout history by the collective actions of social classes in pursuit of their class interests. But up to and including the transition to capitalism, these historical changes brought about through class struggle are not achieved in full consciousness. Men and women make history, but are not full subjects of history. They do not make it knowingly and as they wish, but in alienation. Under capitalism and earlier social forms, men and women are subject to forces which operate like laws of nature, and which escape conscious control. The movement from capitalism to socialism is a movement out of this realm of necessity, to one of freedom: from a state of subjection to impersonal laws, to full human control in the making of society and history. It is the movement in which man's 'species being' is realised. Under capitalism, however, we are still in the realm of necessity, because under capitalism social relations take a reified form. These forms, as we have seen, mask the social reality which they are forms of. Appearance and essence diverge. It is in the collective class interests of the bourgeoisie to take these appearances at full face value, while it is in the interests of the proletariat to penetrate to the essential reality.

The first error, then, of bourgeois theories of knowledge, according to Lukács, is that of *mechanical materialism*. Mechanical materialism recognises that consciousness and knowledge are reflections of reality, but it models this reflection on the image of the mind as a blank page, or as the mirror of a *camera obscura* which mechanically reproduces whatever is presented before it. But the impressions of capitalism which register in the mirror are reflections of its surface appearances not of its essence.

The second error is the polar opposite of the first, that of *idealism*. Idealism correctly perceives that the surface of the forms deceive. But like mechanical materialism, idealism depends on a subject/object dualism. Mechanical materialism reduces the subject to the object, and idealism, the object to the subject. For the idealist, it is consciousness which moulds reality, and not vice-versa. Lukács argues that both theories of knowledge are incorrect, because the true relationship between subject and object is a dialectical one. The tools of knowledge production — theories, scientific laws, methodological practices, etc. — are not the free constructions of human creativity, as the idealist would have it, but objective reflections of that underlying reality (the real world), in its essences rather than its appearances.

It need hardly be said that this is a rather crude sketch of the rich variety of epistemological positions which have been developed since Locke. But Lukács deals in much greater detail than can be indicated here with the history of Western thought; and in any case he is concerned only to map out the limit positions within which that thought is held, rather than to do justice to any particular thinker.

ii. Lukács's Theory of Art

These twin errors of bourgeois thought are repeated in their theories and practices of art, in naturalism and subjectivism respectively. According to Lukács, naturalist art aims at accurate representation of particulars, which for mechanical materialism constitute reality. Subjectivist art takes the opposite term of bourgeois dualism and elevates art as the product of the superior subjective consciousness of the creative artist. Artistic form, free product of that creativity, is elevated above representation as the goal of art, and is seen as the product of genius.

Dialectical materialism, according to Lukács, posits for art and for science the same goal, that of 'showing things as they really are'. All reflection rests upon a contradiction between general and particular, appearance and essence, immediate and conceptual. Each form of reflection has to resolve those contradictions in order to produce knowledge. Lukács differentiates art from science in terms of their different manner of resolving them. Art achieves knowledge of the real through the representation of particulars, where science does so through the discovery of general abstract laws:

> The goal for all great art is to provide a picture of reality in which the contradiction between appearance and reality, the particular and the general, the immediate and the conceptual, etc., is so resolved that the two converge into a spontaneous integrity . . . The Universal appears as a quality of the individual and the particular, reality becomes manifest and can be experienced within appearance. (Lukács, 1970, p34)

Art, in this account, is given considerable privilege. Realist art achieves this magical unity of appearance and essence through *typicality*. This concept, central to Lukács's aesthetics, is legitimised by Engels's use of it, but owes as much to Max Weber as to Engels. Realist art selects for its representations particulars which have this quality of typicality. Through these representations, the real forces and currents which explain social life and history can be displayed. The concept of typicality is elusive, but is fleshed out when the essay 'Narrate or Describe' is taken together with 'Art and Objective Truth'. Lukács argues that realism in the novel requires that characters be shown in action and interaction through the construction of a narrative. The most appropriate type of character, for purposes of 'typicality', is neither the statistical average, nor the 'great hero', but an unexceptional individual caught at the centre of conflicting political and social forces:

> The problem is to find a central figure in whose life all the important extremes in the world of the novel converge and around whom a complete world with all its vital contradictions can be organised. (Ibid., p142)

He gives as his examples the heroes of Scott, such as Morton in *Old Mortality*, and Balzac's Rastignac and Lucien Rubempre. Through the narrative of the strivings of these heroes, the impact of social determinations can be made visible, in a manner which makes it clear that these forces and determinations are a function of 'men' in human relationships. (ibid., p141)

In these narratives, the rules of realism are observed, in that nothing is permitted to happen which might not happen to just such individuals in reality, even though the cumulation of incident and action may be implausible. The validity of the narrative, its realism, does not depend on any one-to-one correspondence between events and characters of the fiction, and those experienced in the real social world. Using the criterion of the statistical average, the cumulation of incidents and the climactic resolutions of the novels of Balzac would, Lukács recognised, be judged unrealistic. Zola, whose concept of typicality, unlike that of Lukács, did refer to the statistical average, complained of Stendhal's work, that 'the truth we encounter every day is abandoned . . . As far as exact truth is concerned, Julien provides me with as many surprises as d'Artagnan.' (Emile Zola in Lukács, 1970, p125) But Lukács argues that it is the narrative structure organised around climax and resolution which constitutes the formal structure of the novel, and it is at this global level of form that correspondence to reality must be sought. In seeking correspondences at the level of incident and character, the naturalists failed to produce the more fundamental correspondence which exists in great realist works between the 'intensive totality' of the work, and the 'extensive totality' of social reality. Flaubert failed to see that like art, life has climaxes and is not the even tenored monotony which it appears to be on the surface:

His belief that 'climaxes' exist only in art and that they are therefore created by artists at will is simply subjective prejudice . . . arising from a superficial observation of . . . the forms life takes in bourgeois society. (Lukács, 1970, p121)

Naturalism, in seeking the statistical average, limits itself to description, as opposed to narration. Narration centres upon human action, because it is through action and interaction that the social world is manifest, and through action that people become interesting to one another. The point of view from which the action is described is that of the participant. Through identification, the reader is drawn into the narrative, by being made to care for the fate of the protagonist. In description, the point of view is that of an uninvolved spectator, and the protagonists become objects for observation rather than figures of identification. Narration centres on action while in naturalism's descriptive realism nothing very much happens. Life flows on with even monotony, interrupted by catastrophes in which the characters are helpless victims. Narration is structured around climaxes which are central to artistic form, but the course of the action is presented always in terms of human intervention and agency.

The criterion for inclusion or exclusion of incident, description, etc., must be, for Lukács, not 'Would this plausibly have happened in reality?' but 'Is this (descriptively plausible) incident required by the dramatic structure of the narrative?' For it is only through the 'intensive totality' of narrative structure that realism is achieved.

Finally Lukács raises the question of audience response. Flaubert wrote that he found his own characters and their lives boring, but felt that this was the inevitable result of descriptive accuracy — most people's lives simply are dull and monotonous; and accuracy is allowed to prevail over narrative interest. Lukács argues that what captures and holds the interest of the reader is always 'the inner poetry of life' — 'the poetry of the turbulent, active interaction of men'. It is in action that men and women are closest to their species being, their essential selves. He associates the rise of detective and other 'worthless' fiction with the rise to dominance of naturalism, on the grounds that where 'great art' fails to provide this satisfying human drama, then other lesser forms will be used to fill the void. Naturalist novels are read out of a sense of duty, but for pleasure people turn to detective fiction.

iii. Art and Politics

Lukács explained the shift from narration to description historically. Prior to 1848, the bourgeoisie was a progressive class, engaged in a positive struggle with the remnants of the old order. The events of 1848, Lukács argued, transformed the bourgeoisie into a reactionary class defending its privileges against the rising proletarian masses. Only in its progressive phase could capitalism generate great progressive art, in which the essence of capitalism could be critically exposed. After 1848, all that was possible for the great artist of integrity was withdrawal into stoicism.

We have seen that in *History and Class Consciousness* the position within the social structure of capitalism from which that structure could become known in its totality was that occupied by the proletariat. Logically it might therefore be expected that the same would be true of knowledge through art — that only those artists who adopted the viewpoint of the proletariat and engaged in its struggles would be capable of producing great realist art. Yet the great art extolled by Lukács was bourgeois art, frequently produced by political reactionaries. Lukács argued that only writers who were in possession of a genuine ideology could produce great works. But the ideology from which the work is produced need not be one which adopts the point of view of the proletariat. Frequently it came from the pens of political reactionaries. Balzac for instance was a monarchist. But Lukács argues that the great writer is a 'partisan for the truth' despite his/her overt ideological commitments. A recent critic of Lukács, Silvia Federici, has complained that this reverses the relationship established in *History and*

Class Consciousness between politics and knowledge (Federici, 1972). In that work, adoption of the viewpoint of the proletariat through active involvement in its political struggles was a condition of realism and truth. In the essays on art, it is the production of realism which places artists on the side of the proletariat, without the inconvenience of actually offering themselves at the barricade. It is honorary membership of the proletariat which the 'great artist' achieves, a particularly painless kind of partisanship. All that the artist is required to do is to 'submit to the dictates of form'. This is a remarkably passive metaphor for a theorist who believes that action is the test of truth. Federici sees it as an abnegation of the revolutionary epistemology of *History and Class Consciousness,* an abject submission to Stalinism, and evidence of Lukács's loss of faith in the proletariat. It may well be all of these things. But if we go back to Lukács's pre-marxist writings, many of the elements of his marxist theory of art are already prefigured, and the contradiction identified by Federici can be located at source.

iv. Lukács's Pre-Marxist Aesthetics

Stedman Jones identifies Lukács's posture in the early decades of this century before his conversion to marxism as what he terms 'the stoicism of the elect' (Stedman Jones, 1971, p42). Left romanticism can provide the basis of a critique of society in the name of culture (Bauman, 1973, pp14–17). The 'elect' are those who, through their participation in this culture, oppose the shoddy reality of capitalism in the name of 'higher' values — what men and women might be, what a truly human society would be like. They are stoical because powerless to transform this vision into reality. Onto this stoicism of the elect and its critique of dehumanised capitalist society, it was very easy to superimpose Marx's theory of commodity fetishism and the concept of reification, and this was precisely the terms of Lukács's conversion to marxism. Lukács's intellectual and political activities in Hungary before and during the abortive Hungarian Soviet Socialist Republic of 1919 have been described in detail and with wit by David Kettler (1971). In accordance with left romanticism, Lukács had seen art as the privileged repository of authentic human values which could no longer find expression in an impoverished, dehumanised capitalist society. In art alone was this capitalist reality denied and refuted. (Here Lukács's analysis comes close to that later developed by the Frankfurt School — the similarities and differences are most illuminating.) Lukács's marxism was superimposed on this left romanticism, leaving much of it intact.

Kettler records the policies of Lukács as Deputy Minister of Culture in the short-lived republic. For Lukács and for those of his circle who followed him into politics and the Communist Party, 'Politics is merely instrumental: culture is the goal.' This (bourgeois) culture had to be transmitted to the proletariat as a central and sacred revolutionary task:

Béla Balázs, head of the section for Art and Literature under Lukács's Ministry, wrote:

> The communist regime feels a great responsibility with regard to which literature is first made available to the proletarian masses, *as yet untouched by any culture.* (Kettler, 1971, p80) (my emphasis)

As Stedman Jones points out, Lukács had traded his pessimistic stoicism of the elect for revolutionary optimism, with his discovery of marxism and the proletariat. For in the latter he thought he had discovered a real force capable of overthrowing capitalism, and creating a social order in which the authentic human ideals preserved against the odds in bourgeois culture could at length be realised, along with the realisation of 'Man's species being'.

Knowledge of the social reality of capitalism emerged, for Lukács, with the rise of the proletariat and the communist movement, and found expression in the writings of Marx and Engels. But knowledge in art predated the proleterian movement and had found expression in the heart of bourgeois culture itself, a culture which owed nothing to the working class and its struggles, but was the product of the progressive phase of the bourgeois revolution. Hence the contradiction identified by Federici. In art there was nothing further for the proletariat to do, except to understand the authentic knowledge and values contained in high bourgeois art, to transmit it in similar works, and to act upon it to transform its vision into the reality of socialism.

Finally, the connection between Lukács's transcending of the 'stoicism of the elect' and his conversion to marxism, and his later hostility to modernism should be noted. For the withdrawal into objectivity and the point of view of the detached observer/scientist for which he criticised naturalism, into the 'inner world' and subjectivity were precisely the options taken by left stoicism, options developed and extended by modernism. In developing his concept of critical realism and attacking modernism, Lukács was in a sense reacting against his own former self.

In the remainder of this chapter, and in the next, I want to examine three different perspectives from which the critique of realism has been mounted. The first is closest to Lukács's realism, for it is premised on the same first principle, that the job of art is 'to show things as they really are'. I shall examine briefly, in this connection, Brecht's critique of Lukács. This critique centres on the conventions of realism, rather than on its goal. Secondly, I shall look at the very different critique which conventionalist marxism has developed. This second critique is more radical than the first, since it challenges the whole concept of a knowable reality, a concept which Brecht shared with Lukács. Brecht's attack on Lukács, and his artistic practice, have been assimilated to this second conventionalist critique of realism, but in my view this assimilation is based on a misunderstanding of Brecht, who was no conventionalist, but a realist like Lukács. Finally, I shall examine a third critique of realism which is neither based on Brecht's critique of the narrow conventions of realism, nor upon the conventionalist questioning of the existence of a knowable reality, but upon a challenge to the realist assertion that the goal of art is 'to show things as they really are'.

3. BRECHT'S CRITIQUE OF REALISM

Brecht's critique of Lukács, and his theory of epic theatre, have been drafted into the service of the conventionalist critique of realism and the celebration of modernism and the avant-garde. But it is important to understand that Brecht's critique was mounted from within an epistemological realism which he shared with Lukács, and from a perspective which accepted the realist goal for art, that of 'showing things as they really are'. Brecht produced no work of marxist theory comparable to Lukàcs's *History and Class Consciousness,* so it is less easy to identify the exact nature of his marxism and his theory of social reality, but it was not Lukàcs's theory of society and history that Brecht opposed. Rather his point of departure from Lukács was the latter's belief that the conventions of realism developed in the nineteenth-century novel were adequate to the task of exposing the nature of society and history in art.

Brecht's essays on Lukács are cryptic, and involve a play on words. (Brecht, 1974) But their import is quite clear. The nature of social reality and the relationship of the audience he was attempting to reach — the working class — to that reality, were such that the techniques and rules of narrative construction developed in the early nineteenth-century novel interfered with the creation of knowledge of that social reality in art, and its transmission to that audience. In particular, it prevented the provocation of that audience beyond knowledge to political action. For instance, the techniques of narration described by Lukács in 'Narrate or Describe' invited, and depended upon, identification by the reader with the protagonist, so that the reader adopted the position of a participant and was drawn into the narrative. Brecht's epic theatre was designed to prevent or at least control such involvement through identification. He preferred to foster a critical detachment on the part of the audience. Paradoxically, the attitude which Brecht wished to provoke is closer to that which Lukács claimed was produced by the descriptive techniques of naturalism — objectivity, detachment, the point of view of a (scientific) observer rather than an emotionally involved participant.

In his essays on Lukács, Brecht attempts to shift the connotations of 'realism', 'formalism' and 'popular'. Realism is, as we have seen, a term which connotes both the attempt to 'show things as they really are' and certain historically developed sets of conventions in art. Brecht separates these two connotations, and retains only the first. He defines realism exclusively in terms of its goal, rather than its conventions. He argues that conventions must be made absolutely subservient to this goal, and that as social reality changes, so different conventions will be appropriate to its depiction. Any approach in art which sticks rigidly to given conventions, whether 'realist' or 'non-realist', regardless of their adaptability to the task of 'showing things as they really are', he calls formalist, and conversely any art which does succeed in this task he calls realist, again regardless of the types of conventions it uses. Realism in art is simply art which reveals the real, whatever conventions it uses, while formalism is art which systematically distorts the real.

Having established these definitions, Brecht is at liberty to argue that the means whereby realism is achieved cannot be determined *a priori* and for all time. There are, he claims, a great many works which are 'realist' in form only, and which are therefore formalist, and vice-versa:

> If someone makes a statement which is untrue — or irrelevant merely because it rhymes, then he is a formalist. But we have innumerable works of an unrealistic kind which did not become so because they were based on an excessive sense of form . . .

> We are then in a position . . . to characterise and unmask as formalistic even works which do not elevate literary form over social content and yet do not correspond to reality. We can even discover such works which are realist in form. There are a great many of them. (Brecht, 1974, p42)

He argues that it is unlikely that conventions of realism developed in relation to nineteenth-century history will prove adequate to changed twentieth-century capitalism. He goes on to confront the problem of capturing and reaching a popular mass audience with works which may need to break with conventions familiar to and popular with that audience. He is deeply concerned to avoid the dilemma that popular forms are usually already colonised for bourgeois ideology, while experimental forms are the preserve of an intellectual élite familiar with the avant-garde. Brecht is absolutely committed to accessibility and popularity in all of his writings. Marxist art must at least be able to hold a mass audience, to be popular, whatever else it requires. At the same time he recognised that new forms are needed which will be unfamiliar and strange. Old ways of receiving pleasure in art may have to be challenged, new ways developed. New ways may depend on *becoming* popular, rather than drawing on existing pleasures. Yet he also insisted that artists be allowed the space to make mistakes, to experiment with new forms.

Brecht's great strength was his recognition that politically effective art

Realism and Marxist Aesthetics II

I. CONVENTIONALISM AND THE CRITIQUE OF REALISM

The second critique of realism which I wish to turn to now comes from marxist conventionalism. Brecht redefined realism in terms of its goal — to show things as they really are. Conventionalist marxism defines realism in art in terms of its second connotation, that is by reference to historically developed conventions of realism. This is because conventionalism challenges the very possibility of the realist goal. There *is* no knowable reality outside of 'signifying practices' and conventions in terms of which that reality is constructed. There is nothing accessible to us with which any given 'signifying practice' can be compared, or to which it can correspond. Ultimately, 'reality' becomes nothing more nor less than the 'signifying practice' itself. Therefore realism is necessarily identified in terms of a particular signifying practice rather than in terms of correspondence to reality. The goal of realism is an illusion. Art cannot 'show things as they really are.'

Hostility to realism is the hallmark of conventionalist marxist aesthetics. Its first premiss is that art is not a mirror to reality, but a construct, produced through a particular type of language use, particular 'signifying practices', particular conventions or rules of construction.

At the outset it should be noted that so far nothing has been said about realism in art which depends upon a denial of this first premiss of anti-realism. The conventionalist critique of realism depends in large part on the attribution to realism of extremely naïve beliefs which very few theorists or practitioners of realism have actually held. Most proponents of realism are acutely aware that art is constructed and that realism, like all other approaches in art, requires conformity to conventions, and depends upon signifying practices.

Because the work of art is constructed out of different materials from the world it represents, the extent to which that representation is 'like' the thing represented must be strictly limited. But this limitation is shared by *any* system of knowledge construction, whether it utilises the language of art, of science, or of common sense. If 'showing things as they really are' required producing their exact replicas, then neither science nor art could aspire to such a goal. Fortunately for realism, in science and in art, this is not a requirement which has to be met. Neither is it necessary to the success of realism in art that the viewer/reader should mistake the art object for what it represents. It is true that *trompe l'oeil* art has sometimes been highly prized, and it is also true that the boundaries between reality and representation are sometimes confused. When Len and Rita married in the British television soap opera, *Coronation Street,* they were showered with wedding presents from viewers. But neither naturalism nor realism depends upon this type of confusion. Most viewers, most of the time, are well aware of the difference between 'The Rovers Return' and their local pub, even though they may well assess the former as a realistic representation of the latter. They are also much more aware than conventionalist critics suppose, or than they themselves can articulate, of the rules which govern this type of representation. The critics' or the viewers' naïve complaint that such and such is 'not realistic' frequently masks a complaint that the rules have been broken.

The attempt to pass itself off for reality is at most a limiting case in realist art. A critique which assumed that this was central to realism's whole project would fail to touch most of its exponents and theorists. Linda Nochlin's study of nineteenth-century realist painting illustrates the extent to which awareness of form and construction was central to them. Their realism consisted in the subordination of these forms to the goal of 'showing things as they really are'. They turned to the methods and findings of the natural sciences of their day for their methods:

> If the Realists, then, did not actually proceed by the methods of natural science, or if they failed to understand its goals adequately, they nevertheless shared in, admired and sought to imitate many of its attitudes and these largely determined the character and quality of their work: impartiality, impassivity, scrupulous objectivity, rejection of *a priori* metaphysical or epistemological prejudice, the confining of the artist to the accurate observation and notation of empirical phenomena, and the description of how, and not why, things happen. (Nochlin, 1971, p43).

This project of a scientific approach to art, and the model of science on which is was based, is clearly positivist, and perhaps some confusion might be avoided if the distinction between epistemological positivism and realism were extended to art. At present movements in the history of art are indiscriminately labelled realist, whether or not they have a realist as opposed to a positivist epistemology.

But even positivist art does not depend upon the mirror fallacy, upon the development of a 'styleless style', a 'simulcrum of reality':

> The commonplace notion that Realism is a 'styleless' or transparent style, a mere simulcrum or mirror image of visual reality is another

barrier to its understanding as an historical and stylistic phenomenon. . . . In painting, no matter how honest or hackneyed the artist's vision may be, the visible must be transformed to accommodate it to the flat surface of the canvas. The artist's perception is therefore conditioned by the physical properties of paint and linseed oil, no less than by his knowledge and technique — even by his choice of brush strokes — in conveying three-dimensional space and form on a two-dimensional picture plane. (ibid., pp14–15).

Far from ignoring form, or the technical possibilities and limitations of his medium, the Realist was acutely aware of them — but as means, not ends in themselves. (ibid., p40).

In fact it is very difficult to find any theorist or critic of any stature making the kinds of assumptions which conventionalism takes to be central to realism. Film is the most likely source for such errors, since the development of photography and the movie camera revived hopes that at last subjectivist bias might be removed and 'reality' allowed to speak for itself. The most influential writer on realism in the cinema is André Bazin. Yet even he cannot easily be pinned down to the naïve view. For instance, in his discussion of Renoir's *La grande illusion* he refers to 'the multiplicity of "realistic inventions"', (Bazin, 1974, p63) through which its realism is achieved, including deep focus, use of camera movements to avoid excessive editing, etc., and comments:

It is through such techniques that Renior attempts to portray realistically the relations between men and the world in which they find themselves. (ibid., p64).

'Realistically' here simply means 'as they are in reality', i.e. 'truthfully' and in no way entails that *an exact replica* of those relations is reproduced in the film. Typically, the realist Bazin emphasises the reality to be portrayed, and the subordination of technique and form to the requirements of 'truth to reality', but this does not entail the 'reproductive fallacy' — the fallacy that the only work which can 'show things as they really are' is a work which is exactly like the reality it represents in every respect, or which creates the illusion of such likeness.

Unlike a fort, an intellectual doctrine should be attacked in its strongest not its weakest form. Attacking straw men (and women) is decidedly bad tactics. Sophisticated and even relatively simple realisms have recognised that the production of works of art which 'show things as they really are' depends on the organisation of materials such as paint, canvas, words, celluloid, etc., which are on the one hand material things and on the other quite unlike the material things which they are used to represent. But once this point has been gained, then the critique of realism must shift onto much more difficult terrain. For if all art, including realist art, depends upon conventions and signifying practices, then realism cannot be singled out either for special praise or blame. Some other grounds must be found for rejecting realism.

In strict logic there is no necessary connection between epistemological realism and realist conventions in art, or between epistemological conventionalism and non-realist art. There is however a *de facto* association.

The conventionalist critique of realism is forced to go beyond the insistence, which realism may readily concede, that realism *constructs* its representations rather than simply *reflecting* the real. It has to defend the more radical view that the goal of representation in art is misplaced, because *no* signifying practice can in principle represent a world which exists outside of that practice. Ultimately, conventionalism in art rests, like epistemological conventionalism, upon the denial of the very category of a knowable external reality.

Conventionalism mounts this case as follows: realism, it is argued, depends on the correspondence theory of truth, upon the ability to compare the assertions of a given language, theory, or 'discourse' with a reality which exists outside that language or discourse. But our only access to this independent reality is via some language, discourse, 'signifying practice' or another. Therefore all that we ever succeed in doing is comparing the terms of one discourse with those of another. Geoffrey Nowell-Smith puts the argument very cogently in his exegesis of the conventionalist position:

> One cannot say 'A woman is . . . ' except by reference to the codes (often conflicting) out of which the concept 'woman' is produced. A 'real' system of reference, which correctly denotes the object referred to, is simply another coded set of signifieds . . . [e.g. in this case, historians' or sociologists' or biologists' codes]. (Nowell-Smith, 1979, p3)

This argument is very similar to that advanced by Hindess and Hirst, and considered in the second chapter, and is answered in the same way when it is raised in relation to the languages of art as it is in the case of the language of science. What is missing is the essential distinction between meaning and *reference*. The concept of a dog cannot bark, it is true any more than the concept of a woman can cook and sew. But it can in both cases *refer* to something in the real world which does do these things. Although we can only talk *about*, or represent, those real things within some signifying practice or another, what is said within those practices depends for its validity not on the signifying practice alone, but on properties and qualities of the things referred to or represented.

It is important to stress the radical implications of the conventionalist critique of realism in art. It cannot be used selectively to undermine the pretensions of an art which claims to 'show things as they really are' without also undermining that goal for *any* 'discourse' including that of science. On the other hand, if the 'real' *is* knowable, then the realist goal is a perfectly proper one for art, and realism in art does not stand self-condemned as ideology. Realism, the goal of showing things as they really are, is only ideological *per se* if *all* attempts to produce knowledge of the real are similarly doomed. There is no stopping point in the conventionalist critique short of a radical conventionalism which denies the existence of a knowable reality. This is why the Hindess and Hirst *reductio* is so valuable. It indicates the positions which must be occupied if conventionalism is to be consistent and rigorous. It is important too to recognise the consequences of drawing back from that position. In art, as in science, any knowledge-claim or truth-claim must first be assessed in terms of 'adequacy to the real' and not short-circuited by drawing attention to its mode of signification. Individual realist works may well be ideological, but this will be by virtue of the actual claims which they make about the real, rather than the way they construct their meanings. Curiously, this is covertly recognised in conventionalist critiques of realist works. Time and again there is an implicit appeal to what we know independently to be the case, to be set against the claims of the realist text that something else is the case.

Finally it must be seen that radical conventionalism does not itself escape the problem of reference. It is forced to do, in the course of its critique of realism, what it claims, as part of that critique, cannot be done, namely, to refer to an external, known world. This may be seen in attempts to describe the realist dilemma and the conventionalist critique. Again, Nowell-Smith's expositon reveals this problem. He uses the well-worn example of the concept 'dog' which cannot bark:

> A crucial tenet of any conventionalism of this kind is the ' "fido"/ FIDO' theory (i.e. the name 'fido' does not bark). (Nowell-Smith, 1979, p2)

'FIDO' in this sentence is capitalised because it refers to an *object* (order of *reference*) an imaginary dog called Fido, rather than to a *name* (order of *concepts*). But what is the status of 'FIDO'? Like 'fido', it consists of a word, and like 'fido' it cannot bark. *No* words bark, but they can be used to *refer* to (imaginary or real) things that do bark. But we can only understand the example if we understand that there are real dogs as opposed to dogs in 'discourse', and that we know various things about their properties and behaviour (even if we know these only *through* discourse). As may be seen in Hindess and Hirst's 'discourse', the rigorous conventionalist position is one which is very difficult, if not impossible, to put into words without assuming the very thing it is concerned to deny — the existence of a knowable world outside of discourse.

The *de facto* connection between conventionalism and non-realist aesthetics follows from the conventionalist denial of the realist belief that there is an external knowable reality which can be made accessible through the construction of works of art. The objection of conventionalism to this realist belief is not that realism suffers from the illusion that it can reproduce this reality unmediated, but ultimately that that external reality can be represented at all, that it is something which is in principle knowable. The conventionalist objection therefore to the conventions of realism is that realism pretends to be able to do something which cannot be done, and that it succeeds in creating the dangerous *illusion* that it *has* succeeded in representing the real, in 'showing things as they really are'.

2. THE CLASSIC REALIST TEXT

An influential version of the conventionalist critique of realism is to be found in the work of Colin MacCabe. His concept of realism is very broad:

> The category of the classic realist text lumps together, in book and film, *The Grapes of Wrath* and *The Sound of Music*, *L'Assommoir* and *Toad of Toad Hall*. (MacCabe, 1974, p12)

This category is defined in terms of two characteristics which all 'classic realist texts' share and by virtue of which they produce 'the reality effect', the illusion that they 'show things as they really are'. Firstly, he claims, such texts consist in a hierarchy of 'discourses' at the apex of which is an unwritten discourse which is privileged. It is this privileged discourse which claims 'adequacy to the real': an authority against which all the other discourses of the text may be measured. In the nineteenth-century novel, before the impact of Flaubert and James made it fashionable to eliminate as far as possible all traces of the intruding author, this privileged discourse was normally that of the author. George Eliot is classic in this respect, and is commonly cited to make the point. Her novels are littered with authorial comment upon action and character, and moral lessons are drawn for the reader in these asides. But the disappearance of the intruding author from the novel did not eliminate the dominant discourse. MacCabe argues that in films, and in novels which lack a narrator or direct authorial comment, the dominant discourse is carried by the structure of the narrative itself. It is when the reader successfully performs the task of unravelling the meaning of the text through the relationship between this dominant discourse and the remaining discourses of the text's hierarchy, and assents to (misrecognises) the 'reality' presented, that the text performs its ideological role.

Secondly, the classic realist text may be identified by the manner in which it 'inscribes' subjects within it — these subjects being author, character, and reader. The classic realist text depends upon identification between imputed reader and character. The moment of ideological recognition — that this is indeed the way things are — only occurs when the reader accepts the position offered by the text. In so doing the reader is constituted as a subject and the work of ideological production is complete.

Thirdly and consequently, the classic realist text is closed. The meanings which it generates are fixed and limited and depend on the reader's acceptance of the position offered by the text. And finally, the constituted reader is passive, the consumer of pre-given meanings, not their active creator.

If the 'signifying practices' of a given literary form define that form, as they do for the conventionalists, then it follows that these practices cannot be simply ignored by 'progressive' or 'revolutionary' writers who wish to write novels or make films but not to reproduce the dominant ideology. They mark out the boundaries within which the form exists.

The commonly preferred solution to this dilemma has been to attempt to undermine these practices from within, by displaying them within the text, instead of disguising them. If a text displays its own signifying practices, then it cannot be mistaken for a 'window on the world'. The illusion of reality will be broken, and the text will be revealed as the producer of ideology. Instead of drawing attention to an external reality which it purports to reveal, the text will draw attention to itself, its own processes of construction. This development is, of course, quite congruent with the conventionalist denial that there *is* a knowable reality outside of discourse. It has the additional advantage of bringing marxist cultural studies into line with modernism, and allowing it to abandon a tradition of realism which has become an embarrassment in the face of the concerns of modernism.

Against the classic realist text is set, then, a 'progressive' or even 'revolutionary' text which bears all the marks of modernism, and is opposed in every respect to the characteristics of the realist text. Where the classic realist text disguises its process of production behind a polished surface which pretends to mirror reality, the progressive text reveals its own construction, its own reality. This has a certain narcissistic effect. The progressive text is always reflexive, concerned with its own processes of signification. (This self-consciousness marks all conventionalism, and the preferred form of conventionalist thought is the auto-critique, as may be seen in both the work of Althusser and of Hindess and Hirst. Conventionalism feeds upon itself.)

Where the classic realist text is closed, allowing the reader only one position from which passively to consume pre-given meanings, the progressive text is open. The reader is forced into the active role of co-producer of meanings, since no privileged reading is offered. (This position has been modified by MacCabe in a subsequent auto-critique. The notion of a single dominant meaning resulting from a single subject-position in the text, has given way to that of the 'preferred reading', and recognition that there is usually more than one position which the reader may take in relation to the text. These concessions to criticism do not materially affect the points which I wish to make here.)

This approach generates a negative attitude towards the products of the mass media, most of which fall within this very catholic category of the classic realist text. By virtue of the need to reach a wide audience, the mass media tend to remain fairly strictly within the bounds of existing signifying practices, and to innovate only with caution. Almost inevitably the media are assessed from this position in the same maner in which they have always been assessed by 'left pessimism' — as purveyors of bourgeois ideology. The wild fantastical of Morecambe and Wise, or the Muppet Show at its anarchic peaks, is distinguished from realist soap opera only to the extent to which each text leaves 'cracks and fissures' on its surface, through which the ideological production may become visible to a critical reading. Interest shifts from popular forms to those works which break with the dominant signifying practices. The avant-garde, not noted despite Brecht's cautious optimism for its appeal to the broad masses, is identified as the source of revolutionary (signifying) practice on the front of ideology.

However, the impact on the conventionalist critique of the cinema has of necessity led to accommodations to and distinctions within popular forms. It has had a double thrust. In addition to its positive engagement with experimental avant-garde cinema, it has shown an interest in and preference for non-realist and highly stylised genres such as melodrama, the western, crazy comedy, etc. Yet this second thrust sits very uneasily with some aspects of the conventionalist critique of realism. All of these are popular forms, and some of them use non-realist conventions. But it is not at all clear that they operate to alert the viewer to the illusions of the realist text, nor that they are not in their own ways classic bourgeois forms, which may or may not be bearers of the dominant ideology. Since the Gothic novel and earlier, some popular genres have depended not upon creating the illusion of reality, but upon a 'willing suspension of disbelief'. The ideological status of these forms can no more be read off from that form than bourgeois ideology can be read off from the form of realism. Crazy comedy is not intrinsically more 'progressive' than conventional realism.

The dilemma which Althusser's theory of ideology and conventionalist aesthetic theory based upon it faces lies in the two equally problematic strategies which are offered. On the one hand, a defensive unmasking of materials accessible to and enjoyed by the working class:

an exposure of 'cracks' and 'fissures' so that the processes whereby they produce the ideological effect can be displayed. And on the other hand, a positive reappraisal of modernism and the avant-garde, the exclusive preserve of and intellectual élite encapsulated within existing social relations. For if popular realist forms reproduce social relations by naturalising them so that they appear necessary and eternal, then they are aided in this ideological task of reproducing existing social relations by the avant-garde, which operates in a different manner but no less effectively. The avant-garde inhabits and arises out of 'structures of feelings and sensibility, whose class co-ordinates are unmistakable'. Behind the language and images of avant-garde art lies a cultural and educational apparatus to which the working class has little access.

It is impossible to produce a truly revolutionary text in a discourse in which only the dominant have any facility. Again, Raymond Williams's strictures against formalism are directly relevant. The question of audience is critical in assessing the politics of a text, and the text's signifying practice must always be related to the requirements and characteristics of that audience as well as to the meanings and effects which it aims to produce.

The conventionalist critique of realism then challenges not only the conventions of realism as did Brecht, but its goal of showing things as they really are. It rests upon the conventionalist denial that there is a knowable external reality which realist art can attempt to reveal; that there *is* any reality beyond the text and its signifying practices to which the text refers. It has led to an élitism in aesthetic practice and theory, and a turning away from certain crucial aspects of Brecht's legacy to marxist aesthetics, his concern for accessibility and popularity. It has moved away from engagement with popular forms, and has opted for one horn of the dilemma of marxist art where Brecht was firmly committed to holding on to both.

3. IS ART A FORM OF KNOWLEDGE?

Finally there is a third position from which realism can be questioned which challenges neither the conventions of realism, nor the realist epistemology on which it is based, the belief in a knowable external reality, but the belief that the goal of art is, or ought to be, to show things as they really are. I will argue that there is nothing in marxist materialism and realism which dictates this goal for art, or the view that art is a form of knowledge.

When the question of the extra-cognitive dimensions and functions of art is raised we move into treacherous territory. I do not wish to suggest that exposure to a work of art is like taking a warm bath, or sinking into emotion. I fully concur with Nelson Goodman's view that 'any picture of aesthetic experience as a sort of emotional bath or orgy is plainly preposterous.' (Goodman, 1969, p245) It would be foolish not to recognise that the goal of using art to expose the real has been a strongly recurrent one, nor that a great deal of knowledge is transmitted through art. To say that art is not a form of knowledge parallel to, but different from, scientific knowledge is not to deny the cognitive content of art. Both marxists (such as Della Volpe) and non-marxists (such as Goodman) have made compelling cases that art is centrally concerned with the production of ideas, and that emotive theories of art cannot even specify the emotive content of a work without reference to its ideas.

i. Art, Ideas and Ideology

But if it is conceded that art does indeed produce ideas, then questions of validity also arise. What I want to argue is that while the ideational content of art may not qualify as knowledge in the full sense, neither is it necessarily relegated to the limbo of ideology. The ideas generated in a work of art may be true or false, adequate or inadequate. The category of 'ideology' cuts across the distinction between the signifying practices of art and of science. In differentiating these practices from one another, we are not isolating a form of signifying practice which is peculiar to ideology. Ideological thinking is to be found in every type of language use. Exposing the ideological foundations of a work of art requires more than an analysis of its signifying practice. Only where the ideas produced using that signifying practice can be shown to be inadequate in respects which touch upon class interest and the class struggle can the work be labelled ideological. And assessment of adequacy cannot be made on the basis of analysis of internal signifying practice alone, but requires referral, in addition to the real properties of the objects of reference of the work.

This claim gains considerable support from the actual analytic practice of marxist critics and theorists, both conventionalist and non-conventionalist. Covert or overt comparisons are constantly made between the work and that to which the work purportedly refers, and the invitation to judge the work as ideological is made in the light of such comparisons. I shall give examples drawn from both realist and conventionalist sources.

Della Volpe is a self-styled rationalist who draws, like conventionalist marxism, upon contemporary linguistic theory. But he is a realist, not a conventionalist, and the use which he makes of these theories is very different from the currents considered here. Della Volpe argues that all cultural forms are forms of thought, all involve conceptual thinking, and all use language. The differences between art, science and common sense, the three main categories which he distinguishes, lie in their different language use. He identifies three main types of concept, the *univocal,* the *equivocal* and the *polysemic,* used by science, common sense and art respectively. The univocal concepts of scientific discourse create a one-to-one relationship between term and concept, equivocal concepts link the same term to different concepts and the same concept to different terms, while polysemic concepts link the same term to a multiplicity of concepts. The common relationship of polysemy and univocality to the equivocal language of ordinary speech allows comparison, translation and interpretation. Art and science are equally intellectual discourses:

> . . .there is a 'poetic discourse' as there is an historical or a scientific discourse . . . a rational and intellectual procedure . . . Poetry (and art in general) is, just like history and science, *concrete reason* . . . *in this it is no different* from history and science in general. (Della Volpe, 1978, p23)

Della Volpe claims of Mayakovsky's poem *Of This Love* that in it:

> The principles of historical materialism and the theoretical and practical themes of Marxism and Leninism are articulated and poetically expressed in metaphor . . . it is not hard to see that Mayakovsky's great poetic strength lies in the brilliant way in which he uses metaphorical and hyperbolic connections to achieve a *typification* of the values of the socialist society in which he lived and of its ideals, institutions and decisive events. (ibid., pp80–1)

Here the invitation to make comparisons between, in this case, poetry and history is overt. But what must be questioned is whether the analysis could be made without access to knowledge developed outside of poetry, in the univocal language of historical analysis. His claim for the poem depends on prior knowledge, shared between reader and analyst, of what those 'values, ideals, institutions and decisive events' in fact consisted in. Such knowledge is, I would maintain, properly developed and validated outside of the discourse of poetry, through analytic and theoretical models of Soviet society and history. If this is the case, then the 'concrete reason' produced in one type of discourse appears to have privilege over that of others, and where poetry (and art in general) stakes its claim upon cognitive grounds — its conceptual rationality — then it also accepts secondary status.

My second example is taken from a quasi-conventionalist analysis — a recent account of the television drama *Days of Hope:*

> . . . the film simply recycles a constant opposition in different terms. This opposition concerns the understanding of class. On the one hand the working class is 'in possession of itself', class conscious, a realised unity of the subject and object of history. On the other hand it is fragmented, alienated, lacking everything (but the good intention) necessary to finally take possession of itself and of history. Therefore

its 'self-knowledge' is abstracted from struggle and turned into its 'nature' . . . (Stevens, 1978, p27)

This interpretation of *Days of Hope* was arrived at through a painstaking and detailed analysis of the imagery and narrative structure of the work, the signifying practices whereby those meanings were created. I am not concerned here with the validity of the interpretation. Rather I want to point out that it depends upon more than is acknowledged, upon a covert invitation to recognise and reject those meanings as inadequate by reference to a knowledge shared again by analyst and reader, but developed quite independently of the work under analysis, of the *real* nature of working-class consciousness and politics. In other words, while interpretation depends on analysis of the work's signifying practice, assessment of its meanings from the point of view of its validity, or of its ideology, depends on comparison between those structures of meaning and their object of reference, through the mediation of another type of discourse.

This implicit appeal to what we already know is ubiquitous and, I would argue, perfectly proper and necessary. It can be seen in much recent feminist criticism mounted from a conventionalist perspective. In an interesting article on images of women, Griselda Pollock explicitly refuses the comparison between 'two separable elements — woman as a gender or social group, versus representations of women' . . . and proposes instead:

> . . . the notion of woman as signifier in an ideological discourse in which one can identify the meanings that are attached to woman in different images and how the meanings are constructed in relation to other signifiers in that discourse. (Pollock, 1977, p26)

Again it is possible to detect the signs of conventionalism — the hint that there *is* no knowable reality outside of discourse; otherwise why is it not permissible to make comparisons between image and reality, between the way in which 'woman' is used as signifier, and women as gender or social group? Two questions arise: by what token are we invited to accept the label of 'ideology' for the discourse she analyses; and how is it to be assessed for its validity? Two contradictory answers are offered, one covert the other overt. The analysis overtly offers an account of the signifiying practices of the discourse in question and shows the ways in which they conceal themselves and pretend to 'show things as they really are'. The images are ideological because they hide their own processes of construction. But covertly the analysis depends on an appeal to beliefs and values shared between reader and analyst, about the position of women in society, the nature of their sexuality, etc. This is knowledge *of* a 'real world' of sex and gender which exists outside of discourse (although it may not exist independently of *all* discourse) and it is, as in the Mayakovsky case, knowledge which was developed outside of the particular discourse under analysis. There is a covert appeal to the 'truths' of the women's movement — our knowledge that the images which are analysed as invitations to rape are violations of the truths, values and aspirations of feminism. The knowledge, beliefs and values of the women's movement are brought to the assessment of the images, and legitimate the label of ideology. Again we are being told on the one hand that any comparison between image and reality is illegitimate, and on the other hand, invited to make precisely such comparisons.

An important point is nevertheless being made by the conventionalists which is often ignored by naïve realist interpretations of media images, etc. Because of the particular, polysemic nature of such images it is easy to mistake the primary referent of the signifier, by identifying only the most immediate, denotative level of reference. For example, if we are to believe some recent psychoanalytic accounts, images of dominant women in Hollywood in the thirties and forties carry the connotation of woman as phallus. This may well be the case, and if so, a level of signification is identified which a realist reading would miss. But one level of connotation does not cancel out another. Whatever else 'woman' as signifier signifies, it *at least* also signifies and refers to women as sex and gender groups. Indeed it is precisely in the relationship between these levels of signification that sexism is located.

To summarise: in so far as art does produce ideas about the social world and history (and much art does) then these ideas may — but need not — be ideological. They are assessable as ideological not by virtue of their 'signifying practice', nor by such tricks as passing themselves off as mirrors of the real, but *by reference to independently acquired knowledge of that to which they refer.* But knowledge production and validation (as opposed to its transmission) is the proper task of science rather than art. Art may express true ideas, and may produce knowledge in the sense that some people may learn these truths through art rather than through historical or sociological analysis. Art may also produce conviction. But the status of its truths *as* valid knowledge is determined elsewhere than in art, in the univocal language of science and history rather than the polysemic language of art.

It follows I think that the cognitive functions of art must be secondary to it. The languages of art and science are very different, as are the ways in which each generates meaning. If the goal of developing knowledge of the external world is what is at stake, then it can hardly be doubted that the methods and the conceptual language of science and history are better adapted to that goal; or at the very least, that they have so successfully staked out their knowledge-claims that any rival claimants necessarily reserve for themselves second-class status, to the extent that they cannot use the methods and signifying practices of science.

The same difficulty attaches to the attempt to define art in terms of the production of 'the ideological effect'. Apart from the fact that it reduces its status even more drastically, even here it is competing with other forms of ideological production which again may be just as good if not better at this task. If art is ideology, ideology is not unique to art. It seems that any attempt to *define* art in terms of its ideas, whether these are held to be intrinsically ideological or not, has the effect of condemning art to play second fiddle to other kinds of intellectual production.

ii. Art, Politics and Pleasure

The attempt to define art in terms of its value in producing knowledge of the real — 'showing things as they really are' — has always faced opposition, but did not come under serious pressure until the advent of prestigious alternative means of achieving that goal with the rise of the sciences. Once science had effectively pre-empted the claim to knowledge, the view of art as knowledge became vulnerable.

In the first instance no necessary clash was anticipated. In eighteenth-century poetry, the early novel and nineteenth-century painting there was at times a close modelling upon the methods of the natural sciences, associated as we have seen with various realist and naturalist movements. As Linda Nochlin shows, nineteenth-century realist painting was self-consciously modelled on a positivist philosophy and methodology of science. Newtonian physics was joyfully celebrated in Augustan poetry. In the case of the early novel the model was more frequently that of the court of law: truthful testimony at first hand is a recurring device for instance in the work of Defoe in the eighteenth century with the birth of the novel, and again in such developments as the adventure/detective fiction of Wilkie Collins in the nineteenth century. *The Moonstone's* narrative is wholly structured around this concept, and risks some pretty dubious narrators and implausible situations in order to maintain it.

But 'the happy marriage of poetry and Newton's Opticks' could not last. The high point of reaction was perhaps Keats' notorious toast: 'confusion to mathematics'. Yet the arts were in no position to mount a hot or even a cold war against the sciences. The politics of peaceful coexistence was the more prudent course, even from the perspective of romantic theory. Much of the aesthetics of Romanticism can be seen as an attempt to stake out independent ground for art, which does not bring it into direct competition with science. Those who continued to make rationalist claims for art did so on the grounds of the different means which art and science adopted in pursuit of the same goal, that of 'showing things as they really are'. Others differentiated them in terms of different objects of knowledge. Science was concerned, it was held, with the objective, external world of things: art with the subjective, inner world of the emotions. This did not entirely solve the problem, since the fledgeling sciences of mind remained as direct competitors, but at least these were less prestigious than contemporary physics. Finally art could be seen as not so much *about* the emotions and the interior, subjective world, as an expression *of* that world. As Abrams has shown, nineteenth-century Romanticism marked a decisive shift from the concern of art with the external world, to concern with the mind of the artist. To see art as the expression of the inner world of the artist was to remove art decisively from the terrain occupied by the sciences.

In addition to expressive theories of art there were and are other sources of extra-cognitive approaches, including theories of art as play, and pragmatic/didactic theories which stress its rhetorical function. Both of the two critiques of realism discussed so far, in this chapter and the last, point beyond cognitive theories even where they themselves remain committed to cognitive rationalism in art. Both, therefore, have something to offer to the third critique, the critique of the realist assumption that art is a form of knowledge.

(a) Conventionalist critique of realism. We have seen that the conventionalist critique has been mounted from the theories developed from three sources; Althusserian marxism, semiology, and Lacanian psychoanalysis. The fundamental basis of all three is a conventionalist theory of language. The overall tone is highly rationalist, and might seem to be a far cry from romantic/expressive theories of art. The link is through the third contribution, psychoanalysis.

Romantic theory identified the source and origin of art in the spontaneous overflow of the emotions. As such, it was felt to be beyond conscious control, emanating as it did from an unconscious layer of the mind. Modern psychoanalytic interpretations of films and literature are infinitely more sophisticated. Yet cultural products are still analysed as expressions of the work of the unconscious. The pleasure of the text is seen as a function of the relationship of the work of art to unconscious desires.

Of the three sources of conventionalism in cultural studies, this latter one is the most interesting from the present point of view. While Lacan's work is based on conventionalism, Freud's is not. However, the uses of psychoanalytic theory in the interpretation of texts will be subject to the same limits and weaknesses as the theory itself. In Chapter 2 I argued that one major limitation of both Freudian and Lacanian theory lay in their inadequate theorisation of female sexuality. The effects of this lack can be seen in several of the recent works of psychoanalytic interpretation of film. The 'figures of desire' which such works identify in film imagery usually cluster around images of women, while the place of the female spectator is completely disregarded. The imputed viewer of these films is, on this analysis, the male as voyeur. Women figure only as objects of male desire. This is as true of feminist analyses as it is of the work of male Lacanians.

Secondly, I argued that Freud and Marx cannot be synthesised in any simple fashion. But despite these qualifications I believe that the psychoanalytic approach pinpoints a layer of meaning in art which is crucially concerned with desire, repression, wish-fulfilment, etc., rather than with the development of knowledge about the external, public social world. To this extent the approach through psychoanalysis, whether in the work of the Lacanians or in Surrealism, is of great importance. It points beyond the fetters of cognitive rationalism, even if it raises almost as many problems as it solves.

(b) Brechtian Critique of Realism: Art and Politics. The Brechtian critique of Lukács's theory of realism was mounted, as we have seen, from within realism itself — the goal of showing things as they really are. Yet Brecht too, despite his rationalism, points beyond cognitive realism in some respects. Brecht drew upon another tradition than that of realism in art, that of pragmatic/didactic theory. This tradition viewed art in terms of the harnessing of pleasure to learning. Brecht's concept of 'cheerful and militant learning' places him fair and square within this tradition. Again this points beyond the level of ideas in art, because in order to subordinate pleasure to learning, those pleasures must first be identified. And while I do not wish to under-estimate or deny the intellectual pleasures afforded by art yet it would be surprising if these were the only or even the main pleasures offered by works of art and entertainment.

Brecht's attitude towards pleasure in art was always ambivalent. It was to serve learning rather than to be valued in its own right. And where it might prejudice learning it was not to be indulged. Hence his refusal of the pleasure of identification. Despite his insistence on the importance of art as entertainment, he was a rationalist. Political action — participation in the class struggle — was not to be produced through exciting feelings of solidarity, moral outrage, commitment, sympathy with oppression, indignation at exploitation and unnecessary suffering. It was to be mediated by thought not feeling. The audience must be forced to stand back from the emotional response produced by the work, to contemplate what it saw, to coolly assess its own relationship to the spectacle. This same rationalism informs much conventionalism and is the true legacy of Brecht which conventionalism has inherited. The processes and manipulations to which we are subject when the work of art produces the ideological effect must become a matter of conscious inspection, so that we may escape those effects. Similarly, progressive or revolutionary texts are essentially texts which make us think rather than texts which indulge us in pleasures. The rhetoric of making the consumer, the audience/reader, into a producer of meanings, of making the audience work, is a rhetoric based upon one kind of work, the intellectual labour of thinking. Resistance to this particular strand of puritanism is not to be conflated with anti-intellectualism. It is simply to deny that pleasure is or ought to be always at the service of knowledge, and that politics is only served by pleasure through the mediation of knowledge.

This leaves an area in which little work has been done, which touches upon questions of pleasure of a kind which neither the psychoanalytic nor the Brechtian approach touch: social pleasures. The pleasures of a text may be grounded in pleasures of an essentially public and social kind. For instance, pleasures of common experiences identified and celebrated in art, and through this celebration, given recognition and validation; pleasures of solidarity to which this sharing may give rise; pleasure in shared and socially defined aspirations and hopes; in a sense of identity and community. These social pleasures have long been recognised, for instance in the Durkheimian tradition in sociology. This tradition is politically conservative, and the social pleasures themselves may certainly be mobilised for reactionary politics. Like the desires of the unconscious, they are not in themselves either progressive or reactionary; but a political aesthetics, which marxist aesthetics must be, ignores this dimension at its peril. Richard Dyer's work on utopianism in popular entertainment is of great interest from this point of view (Dyer, 1978). Otherwise this is a neglected area which marxist cultural studies, conventionalist and realist alike, have ignored.

While all of these sources of pleasure in the text are of unquestionable importance, they are none of them specific to art. Unconscious desires are figured elsewhere, in dreams and in symbolic action, and solidarity and commitment, the sharing of experience, also take more direct forms. The discerning of aesthetic form itself must be seen as a major source of pleasure in the text — the identification of the 'rules of the game', and pleasure in seeing them obeyed, varied and even flouted. These are learned pleasures, and they touch on differences of class and sex in ways that have yet to be explored. Aesthetic sensibilities are class- and sex-linked, and the politics of aesthetic pleasure will depend on the particular ways in which that sensibility has been appropriated and developed along lines of sex and class.

In this final chapter I have attempted to look at some of the areas which marxist aesthetics might explore, without losing its essential political component, but taking it beyond the narrow cognitive rationalism by which it has been largely bound. I have looked at the critiques of realism negatively, in terms of the ways in which they have remained caught within that cognitive rationalism, and positively in terms of the various ways in which they transcend it and point in another direction.

Conclusion

This work has investigated certain contemporary developments in marxist cultural studies from the point of view of their contribution towards the development of a sociology of art and entertainment, that is to say, an approach which places them within their socio-historical context, and views them as social phenomena. I have concentrated on marxist cultural studies for several reasons. Firstly, as indicated in the introduction, it is marxism which has made virtually all the running in this project of sociology of art. Secondly, there has been a tremendous resurgence of interest in marxism generally in the past decade and a half, and thirdly, a push from within cultural studies towards the sociological context. All of these factors have led to a renewal of marxist cultural studies, and a turning to marxism on the part of cultural studies.

It would be a mistake to jump upon this particular bandwagon uncritically, without recognising the extent and seriousness of the theoretical and empirical problems which marxism confronts. Equally it would be a mistake to think that other strands of the sociological tradition can be safely ignored. But despite these qualifications, and in full recognition of the work still to be done — for as Pierre Vilar has said, marxist history is a history in the making — I believe that marxist theory and method has given us an approach to the understanding and explanation of society and history which remains unmatched.

Marxism is, of course, not simply an intellectual doctrine but also a politics. In this it does not depart as far as is commonly supposed from the remainder of classical sociology. No doctrine has been more widely misunderstood or abused than Max Weber's doctrine of value-freedom for sociology. His occasional essays (Weber, 1948) as well as his more turgid and difficult methodological writings make it clear that while (social) science cannot answer the question 'what shall I do, how shall I live?', the whole point of developing such a science is in the service of politics and ethics. While the social scientist, in his/her professional role, ought not, according to Weber, to suffer political and ethical judgements and action to enter into their work, he would have considered a social scientist who was not *also* deeply concerned with such judgements and actions a curious animal indeed. So while it is true that the relationship between theory, politics and action is very different for Marx and Weber, each is equally concerned with the links between these things. Marxist and Weberian politics are quite different, but to suppose that what differentiates Marxism from Weberianism is that one contains a politics and imperatives for action while the other does not, is func ..ınentally to misunderstand both Weber's work, and much contemporary politics.

Marxism is a theory of history, whose materialism, I have argued, consists in the principle of the primacy of the mode of production in determining both the structure of the social order and the conditions of effective political intervention in shaping and directing its history.

The marxist theory of the capitalist mode of production does not as such have anything very specific to say about art and entertainment, however, and the value of trying to adapt marxist categories, method and theory to the disciplines of cultural studies might be questioned. While marxism cannot brook a specialist economics without sociology, or vice-versa, clearly there *are* specialised disciplines concerned with phenomena such as language and art which must develop concepts and theories appropriate to their object. While marxism pushes towards an understanding of the interconnection between various social phenomena, it does not and cannot exercise the kind of intellectual hegemony which would allow it to subordinate each and every specialist area of enquiry to its broad categories of theory and method. Yet neither can marxists who are also specialists in such fields complacently ignore the potential and actual contradictions between marxist theory of history and those specialised disciplines, for two reasons.

Firstly, art is a social phenomenon. That is to say, it is produced and consumed within particular social relations, it depends upon particular social conditions, and has particular social consequences. Any attempt to theorise one or more of the arts, or art in general, will also carry along with that theory an implicit or explicit sociology, as the history of aesthetics amply testifies. If the account given of the sciences in the first chapter of this work is even approximately correct, then the requirement of consistency and coherence obtains between adjacent disciplines as well as within each specialism. No marxist specialist in cultural studies could therefore afford to tolerate in the long run a situation where, within that specialism, assumptions were being made about the nature of society and social interaction which were diametrically opposed to those made within the marxist theory of history.

Secondly, *marxist* cultural studies is precisely the study of the intersection of society, art and politics in particular historical conjunctures, so that the social and political context of art is no longer a question of background assumptions, but brings these questions very much to the forefront of the whole enterprise.

It follows, however, that marxist cultural studies is a hybrid, which must draw no less upon specialist aesthetic theories than upon marxism. One concern of this work has been that those theories on which contemporary marxist cultural studies has drawn, in semiology and Lacanian psychoanalysis, are theories whose sociological and methodological assumptions are conventionalist, and that this conventionalism has been matched by developments within marxism itself, in the work of Althusser and the post-Althusserians, which take marxism successively further along the road from realism to conventionalism.

A second major concern of this work has been the strong association of marxist cultural studies prior to this conventionalist intervention, with an aesthetics of realism. The social context of art and entertainment is a question of two types of relationship, that of cause and that of meaning. But whether the chief focus had been the social cause-effect nexus within which the production and consumption of art and entertainment is caught, or the relationship which obtains between the meanings produced by the work and the real social world to which these meanings in part refer, marxist cultural studies have been most at home with an aesthetics and practice of realism. The current of conventionalist marxist cultural studies has been liberating in its effect of breaking decisively the link which binds and restricts marxism to a realist aesthetic, but it has achieved this break at the expense of marxism's realist epistemology, and at the cost of an élitism which has been the result of the conflation of this shift from realism to modernism, with a parallel shift from popular and mass art to the avant-garde.

I have attempted to show in this work that the epistemological realism which is an essential defining feature of marxist thought does not tie marxism to a realist aesthetics. Realism in the arts has also been associated with cognitive rationalism — an emphasis on the knowledge and learning functions of art and entertainment in its relationship to politics, rather than upon extra-cognitive dimensions. The convention-list critique of realism, and Brecht's critique from within realism, remain trapped within the boundaries of cognitive rationalism even where they each in their different ways point beyond those boundaries. I have argued that cognitive rationalism is in no way implicated in marxist realism and materialism, and have tried to indicate possible avenues of development for a marxist aesthetics which is not tied to rationalism, but which retains its link with politics and the popular and pleasurable.

It follows that marxist cultural studies will necessarily find itself engaged with a variety of strands of aesthetic theory which are apparently very distant from the concern of marxism. These will include psychoanalytic approaches, theories of art as play, pragmatic theories, etc. Many of these avenues have already been opened up by conventionalist marxist cultural studies, to its credit. But it need hardly be said that such sources cannot be taken over wholesale and exploited for purposes of marxist cultural studies just as they stand, for many of them are incompatible with marxism. The theoretical and practical work of marxist cultural studies will involve the transformation of these theories as they become resources in that work, so that in the form in which they are used they will probably bear as much and as little resemblance to their origins as marxism bears to political economy.

This work of the development of marxist cultural studies is work in progress, and it is no part of the programme to simply transfer and apply ready-made concepts and theory from one field, the study of history, to another. As Pierre Vilar might also have said, marxist aesthetics and cultural theory is a theory in the making.

References

Abrams, M. H., *The Mirror and the Lamp*, OUP, Oxford 1953.

Althusser, L., *For Marx*, New Left Books, London 1977(a).

Althusser, L., *Lenin and Philosophy and Other Essays*, New Left Books, London 1977(b).

Althusser, L. and Balibar, E., *Reading Capital*, New Left Books, London 1977.

Balibar, E. and Macherey, P., 'Littérature comme forme idéologique', in *Littérature*, No. 13, 1974.

Baudry, J-L., 'The Apparatus', *Camera Obscura*, No. 1, 1976.

Bauman, Z., *Culture as Praxis*, Routledge and Kegan Paul, London 1973.

Bazin, A., *Jean Renoir*, W. H. Allen, London 1974.

Bellour, R., 'Le blocage symbolique', *Communications* 23, Paris 1975, abridged and translated in *Psychoanalysis/Cinema/Avant-Garde*, Edinburgh '76 Magazine, 1976.

Benton, T., *Philosophical Foundations of the Three Sociologies*, Routledge and Kegan Paul, London 1977.

Bhaskar, R., 'Feyerabend and Bachelard', *New Left Review*, No. 94, 1975.

Brecht, B., 'Against Georg Lukács', *New Left Review*, No. 84, 1974. (Reprinted in Bloch, E., *et al.*, *Aesthetics and Politics*, New Left Books, London 1978.)

Cahiers du Cinéma, collective text, 'John Ford's *Young Mr. Lincoln*', No. 223, 1970, translated in *Screen*, Vol. 13, No. 3, 1972 and *Screen Reader 1*, SEFT, London 1977.

Clarke, S., *et al.*, *One-Dimensional Marxism*, Allison and Busby, London 1980.

Della Volpe, G., *Critique of Taste*, New Left Books, London 1978.

Dyer, R., 'Entertainment and Utopia', *Movie*, No. 24, 1978.

Federici, S., 'Notes on Lukács's Aesthetics', *Telos*, No. 11, 1972.

Freud, S., *On Sexuality*, Penguin Books, Harmondsworth 1977.

Goodman, N., *The Languages of Art*, OUP, London 1969.

Hall, S. and Whannel, P., *The Popular Arts*, Hutchinson, London 1964.

Harre, R., *The Philosophies of Science*, OUP, London 1972.

Hindess, B. and Hirst, P. Q., *Mode of Production and Social Formations*, Macmillan, London 1977.

Hirst, P. Q., *Problems and Advances in the Theory of Ideology*, Communist Party Pamphlet, Cambridge 1976.

Hite, S., *The Hite Report*, Talmy, Franklin, London 1977.

Jameson, F., *The Prison-House of Language*, Princeton U.P., Princeton 1972.

Keat, R. and Urry, J., *Social Theory as Science*, Routledge and Kegan Paul, London 1975.

Kettler, D., 'Culture and Revolution: Lukács in the Hungarian Revolution of 1918' *Telos*, No. 10, 1971.

Lukács, G., *History and Class Consciousness*, Merlin Press, London 1968.

Lukács, G., *Writer and Critic*, Merlin Press, London 1970.

MacCabe, C., 'Realism and the Cinema', *Screen*, Vol. 15, No. 2, 1974.

Mandel, E., *Late Capitalism*, New Left Books, London 1972.

Marx, K., *The 18th Brumaire of Louis Napoleon, Selected works*, Vol. 1, FLPH Moscow 1962.

Marx, K., *Capital*, Vols. I and II, Lawrence and Wishart, London 1970.

Marx, K., *Grundrisse*, Penguin Books, Harmondsworth 1973.

Molina, V., 'Notes on Marx and the Problem of Individuality', *Working Papers in Cultural Studies*, No. 10, 1977: *On Ideology*.

Nochlin, L., *Realism*, Penguin Books, Harmondsworth 1971.

Nowell-Smith, G., 'Why Realism?' BFI Summer School Papers, 1979, unpublished.

Pollock, G., 'What's Wrong with Images of Women?' *Screen Education*, No. 24, 1977.

Stedman Jones, G., 'The Marxism of the Early Lukács', *New Left Review*, No. 70, 1971.

Stevens, T., 'Reading the Realist Film', *Screen Education* No. 26, 1978.

Thompson, D., *(ed.)*, *Discrimination and Popular Culture*, Penguin Books, Harmondsworth 1964.

Weber, M., 'Politics as a vocation' and 'Science as a vocation', in Gerth, H. H. and Wright Mills, C., *(eds.)*, *From Max Weber*, Routledge and Kegan Paul, London 1948.

Williams, R., *Keywords*, Fontana, London 1976.

Williams, R., 'Realism and Non-Naturalism', *Edinburgh International Television Festival 1977*, Official Programme, *Broadcast*, 1977.

Further Reading

This work is aimed primarily at people who are reasonably familiar with current debates in marxist cultural studies, but I hope it will also be of interest more widely: for example, to sociologists who may be less familiar with those developments, while they may be more familiar than students of film literature, etc., with the debates in philosophy of science referred to here. Because readers may come from such disparate backgrounds, I thought it might be useful to include further reading in relation to each area covered in the work, so that that background may be filled out as appropriate. This is not intended to be a comprehensive bibliography. In each of the areas covered there are bibliographical guides readily available elsewhere.

I. RECENT DEBATES IN PHILOSOPHY OF SCIENCE

There is a great deal of literature in the philosophy of science which comes from an empiricist perspective, or which describes and analyses empiricism. The three sources which I have drawn upon most heavily in this work each have extensive sections on empiricism and positivism.

KEAT, R. and URRY, J., *Social Theory as Science,* Routledge and Kegan Paul, London 1975.

This work is organised analytically. It is uneven in quality, but the sections in the first half on positivism, realism and conventionalism are very clear.

BENTON, T., *Philosophical Foundations of the Three Sociologies,* Routledge and Kegan Paul, London 1977.

This work is in some respects more satisfactory. It attempts to deal with the issues in historical perspective.

BHASKAR, R., *A Realist Theory of Science,* Harvester Press, Brighton 1978.

I have drawn heavily upon Bhaskar's defence of realism in science, but this is not an introductory text, and presupposes familiarity with the issues and debates in philosophy of science. It also deals almost exclusively with the natural sciences, whereas both of the other two texts are primarily concerned with the social sciences. The implications of a philosophy of realism for the social sciences are by no means obvious. For example, Rom Harré, one of the pioneers of modern realist philosophy of science, has used realism to sponsor and legitimate a variant of sociological phenomenology which is about as far removed as it is possible to be from the marxism shared by the three realist texts considered here. Bhaskar has recently published a companion volume on the social sciences:

BHASKAR, R., *The Possibility of Naturalism: a Philosophical Critique of the Contemporary Human Sciences,* Harvester Press, Brighton 1979.

Debates in the philosophy of social science, since the early sixties, have been dominated by the challenge to positivist social science which came from contemporary linguistic philosophy. The most influential work in this country was:

WINCH, P., *The Idea of a Social Science and its Relation to Philosophy*, Routledge and Kegan Paul, London 1958.

Following Wittgenstein, Winch argued that human action and interaction were rule-governed activities which were bounded by language, and subject to interpretive understanding rather than scientific explanation. Each society was unique to the extent that its language and culture were unique and comparisons could not be made across cultures. Because of his stress upon language, it is interesting to compare Winch and his follwers with modern marxist conventionalism. Despite their very different theories and politics, they share many similar problems. For a representative sample of the debates around interpretive sociology and the philosophy of action, see:

WILSON, B.R. (*ed.*), *Rationality*, Blackwells, Oxford 1973.

LASLETT, P. and RUNCIMAN, W. G. (*eds.*), *Philosophy, Politics and Society*, Second Series, Oxford 1962.

EMMET, E. and MacINTYRE, A. (*eds.*), *Social Theory and Philosophical Analysis*, Macmillan, London 1970.

Benton and Keat and Urry each have sections which discuss these issues.

One of the most important debates in philosophy of science in recent years has centred around the work of the conventionalist Thomas Kuhn and the reaction to that work of Karl Popper and his associates. The Popper/Hempel orthodoxy which dominated philosophy of science until recently is best represented in the following:

POPPER, K. R., *The Logic of Scientific Discovery*, Hutchinson, London 1974.

This is the *locus classicus*. But Popper's work is also interesting in its political and ideological context, and this is best revealed in more polemical works such as:

POPPER, K. R., *The Poverty of Historicism*, Routledge and Kegan Paul, London 1960.

POPPER, K. R., *The Open Society and its Enemies*, Routledge and Kegan Paul, London 1962.

Hempel's covering law model of scientific explanation is clearly set out in:

HEMPEL, C., *Philosophy of Natural Science*, Prentice-Hall, Hemel Hempstead 1966.

Kuhn's conventionalist challenge first appeared in 1962 in:

KUHN, T. S., *The Structure of Scientific Revolutions*, University of Chicago Press, Chicago 1970.

The subsequent debate between Kuhn and the Popperians can be found in:

LAKATOS, I. and MUSGRAVE, A. (*eds.*), *Criticism and the Growth of Knowledge*, Cambridge University Press, Cambridge 1970.

One contributor to that debate was Paul Feyerabend. He shifted from Popperian orthodoxy to radical Kuhnianism and beyond, and his work has received considerable attention from conventionalist marxists.

FEYERABEND, P. K., *Against Method: Outline of an Anarchist Theory of Knowledge*, Cambridge University Press, Cambridge 1978.

See also:

BHASKAR, R., 'Feyerabend and Bachelard', *New Left Review*, No. 94, 1978.
On realism, see also:
HARRE, R., *Philosophies of Science: An Introductory Survey*, Oxford University Press, Oxford 1972.

2. MARXISM, REALISM AND MATERIALISM

Both Benton and Keat and Urry include sections on marxism as a realism, although Keat and Urry are, in my view, weakest in their discussion of marxism. Benton identifies marxist realism with Althusserianism, but his critical interpretation of Althusser pushes that identification to its limits.

A collection of essays has recently appeared which covers the relevant issues:
MEPHAM, J. and RUBEN, D. H. (*eds.*), *Issues in Marxist Philosophy* (3 vols.), Harvester Press, Brighton 1979.
There is nothing entirely satisfactory on the question of materialism.
TIMPANARO, S., *On Materialism*, New Left Books, London 1976.
This consists of a collection of polemical essays of uneven quality. The most interesting, for its challenge to the anti-materialism of much contemporary linguistics, is the essay entitled 'Structuralism and its Successors'.

For the work of Marx himself, there is in the end no substitute for the original texts. Reading *Capital* is, of course, a major undertaking and is best attempted collectively in a reading group. Some useful secondary sources include:
SWEEZY, P. M., *Theory of Capitalist Development*, Monthly Review, New York 1962.
FINE, B., *Marx's 'Capital'*, Macmillan, London 1975.
RUBIN, I., *Essays on Marx's Theory of Value*, Black and Red, Detroit 1972.
There are a number of Marx readers, the best of which is probably still:
BOTTOMORE, T. and RUBEL, M. (*eds.*), *Karl Marx: Selected Writings in Sociology and Social Philosophy*, Penguin, Harmondsworth 1970.
Recent feminist theoretical work has pointed to the failure of marxism to take sufficient account of sex as well as class oppression and the need to rework marxist theory in the light of this omission. See, for example:
BARRETT, M., *Women's Oppression Today: Problems in Marxist Feminist Analysis*, New Left Books, London 1980.

3. ALTHUSSER'S THEORY OF KNOWLEDGE AND IDEOLOGY

Since Althusser has continuously subjected his work to self-criticism, it is important to read it chronologically in order to gain some sense of its development. His writings on knowledge production are found in the main in his early essays:
ALTHUSSER, L., *For Marx*, New Left Books, London 1977.
ALTHUSSER, L. and BALIBAR, E., *Reading 'Capital'*, New Left Books, London 1977.
There are two essays on ideology in *For Marx*, but the most influential essay on this topic is undoubtedly 'Ideology and Ideological State Apparatuses' in:

ALTHUSSER, L., *Lenin and Philosophy and Other Essays,* New Left Books, London 1977.
More recently Althusser has published his auto-critique:
ALTHUSSER, L., *Essays in Self-Criticism,* New Left Books, London 1976.

The critical literature on Althusser is large and growing. Among the best known and most influential are:
GLUCKSMANN, A., 'A Ventriloquist Structuralism' *New Left Review,* No. 72, 1972.
GERAS, N., 'Althusser's Marxism: an Account and Assessment,' *New Left Review,* No. 71, 1972.
CALLINICOS, A., *Althusser's Marxism,* Pluto Press, London 1976.
More recently, E. P. Thompson's polemical essay has had considerable impact:
THOMPSON, E. P., *The Poverty of Theory,* Merlin Press, London 1979.
Other critical essays of importance are:
RANCIÈRE, J., 'On the Theory of Ideology', *Radical Philisophy,* Vol. 7, No. 19, Spring 1978.
CLARKE, S., 'Althusserian Marxism' in Clarke *et al., One-Dimensional Marxism,* Allison and Busby, London 1980.
VILAR, P., 'Marxist History: a History in the Making', *New Left Review,* No. 80, 1975.

For an introduction to the work of Hindess and Hirst, and the post-Althusserians, see:
HINDESS, B. and HIRST, P. Q., *Pre-capitalist Modes of Production,* Routledge and Kegan Paul, London 1977.
HINDESS, B. and HIRST, P. Q., *Mode of Production and Social Formation,* Macmillan, London 1977.
HIRST, P., *Problems and Advances in the Theory of Ideology,* Communist Party Pamphlet, Cambridge 1976.
HIRST, P., 'Althusser's Theory of Ideology' *Economy and Society,* No. 5, Routledge and Kegan Paul, London 1976.
The journals *Economy and Society, Ideology and Consciousness* and *M/F* come from post-Althusserian perspectives.

The theory of the subject, appropriated from Lacan by Althusser, has occasioned interpretations that are frequently as difficult to understand as the original. Some of Lacan's writings have appeared in translation, including:
LACAN, J., *Four Fundamental Concepts of Psychoanalysis,* Hogarth, London 1977.
LACAN, J., *Ecrits: a Selection,* Tavistock Publications, London 1977.
For works which explain and/or use Lacan's theory, see:
ALTHUSSER, L., 'Freud and Lacan', *New Left Review,* No. 55, 1969.
COWARD, R., 'Lacan and Signification', *Psychoanalysis/Cinema/Avant-Garde, Edinburgh '76* Magazine, 1976.
COWARD, R. and ELLIS, J., *Language and Materialism,* Routledge and Kegan Paul, London 1977.
For critical reviews of Lacanianism, see:
WOLLHEIM, R., *New York Review of Books,* Vol. XXV, Nos. 21—2, January 1979.

RÉE, J., 'Marxist Modes', *Radical Philosophy*, No. 23, 1979.
There are a number of relevant articles in *M/F*.
Of particular interest to feminists is the work of Lacan's erstwhile colleague
Luce Irigaray; also the work on 'semiotics' of Julia Kristeva:
IRIGARAY, L., 'Women's Exile', *Ideology and Consciousness*, No. 1, 1977.
KRISTEVA, J., 'Signifying Practice and Mode of Production',
Psychoanalysis/Cinema/Avant-Garde, Edinburgh '76 Magazine, 1976.

4. ON IDEOLOGY

There is an enormous literature on the subject of ideology. A good introduction
and overview may be found in:
HALL, S., 'The Hinterland of Science: Ideology and the "Sociology of
Knowledge" ', *Cultural Studies*, No. 10, 1977.

See also:
LICHTHEIM, G., *The Concept of Ideology and Other Essays*, Vintage, New York
1974.
On Gramsci:
HOARE, Q. and NOWELL-SMITH, G. (*eds.*), *Prison Notebooks*, Lawrence
and Wishart, London 1973.
HALL, S., LUMLEY, B. and McLENNAN, G., 'Policies and Ideology:
Gramsci', *Cultural Studies*, No. 10, 1977.
BOGGS, C., *Gramsci's Marxism*, Pluto Press, London 1976.
ANDERSON, P., 'The Antinomies of Antonio Gramsci', *New Left Review*, No.
100, 1976.
In the mid-sixties a debate took place between Anderson and E. P. Thompson
which partly hinged on Anderson's use of Gramsci's concepts in his analysis of
British society since the Civil War.
ANDERSON, P., 'Origins of the Present Crisis', *New Left Review*, No. 23,
1964, printed in ANDERSON, P. and NAIRN, T., *Towards Socialism*,
Fontana, London 1965.
THOMPSON, E. P., 'Peculiarities of the English', *Socialist Register 1965*,
Merlin Press, London 1965.
The work of the *Centre for Contemporary Cultural Studies* has been greatly informed
by Gramsci's thought—see back numbers of *Cultural Studies*.

On political economy and ideology, see, for a discussion of commodity fetishism
and the theory of ideology:
MEPHAM, J., 'The Theory of Ideology in *Capital*', *Cultural Studies*, No. 6,
1974.
For criticism of the attempt to construct a theory of ideology from the concept of
commodity fetishism, written from a post-Althusserian perspective:
ROSE, N., 'Fetishism and Ideology', *Ideology and Consciousness*, No. 2, 1977.
The journal *Media, Politics and Society* approaches media studies from the
perspective of political economy, as does the work of Golding and Murdock:
MURDOCK, G. and GOLDING, P., 'For a Political Economy of Mass
Communications', *Socialist Register 1973*, Merlin Press, London 1973.

i. General

There are a number of useful anthologies which can provide an introduction to the ways in which marxists have approached aesthetic questions:

LANG, B. and WILLIAMS, F. (*eds.*), *Marxism and Art: Writings in Aesthetics and Criticism*, McKay, New York 1962.

BAXANDALL, L. (*ed.*), *Radical Perspectives in the Arts*, Penguin, New York 1972.

CRAIG, D. (*ed.*), *Marxists on Literature: an Anthology*, Penguin, Harmondsworth 1975.

There have also been a number of introductions to marxist aesthetics in recent years. None is particularly satisfactory and all, of course, are written from particular standpoints, even where they attempt a neutral survey.

LAING, D., *The Marxist Theory of Art*, Harvester Press, Brighton 1978.

EAGLETON, T., *Marxism and Literary Criticism*, Methuen, London 1976.

JAMESON, F., *Marxism and Form: Twentieth-Century Dialectical Theories of Literature*, Princeton University Press, Princeton 1971.

These all attempt to survey the major marxist approaches to art and literature.

WILLIAMS, R., *Marxism and Literature*, Oxford University Press, Oxford 1977.

This is organised around concepts and issues which have informed marxist approaches to literature, and is illuminating for Williams' own relation to marxist approaches.

ii. Raymond Williams

The best introduction to Williams' thought as it has developed and changed over the years is:

WILLIAMS, R., *Politics and Letters*, New Left Books, London 1979.

This takes the form of a lengthy interview.

On realism:

WILLIAMS, R., *Keywords*, Fontana, London 1976.

WILLIAMS, R., 'Realism and Non-Naturalism', *Edinburgh International Television Festival* 1977, Official Programme, *Broadcast*, 1977.

WILLIAMS, R., 'A Lecture on Realism' *Screen*, Vol. 18, No. 1, 1977.

For a good example of Williams' approach to literature, see:

WILLIAMS, R., *The Country and the City*, Chatto and Windus, London 1973.

Williams' ex-student, Eagleton, has written a critical essay which attempts to place Williams within his own 'great tradition'. It appears in:

EAGLETON, T., *Criticism and Ideology*, New Left Books, London 1976.

But the most illuminating discussion of Williams' work is his own, in response to interview questions, in *Politics and Letters*.

iii. Georg Lukács

Despite his own critical distance from it, as expressed in the introduction to the English translation:

LUKÁCS, G., *History and Class Consciousness: Studies in Marxist-Dialectics*, Merlin Press, London 1975,

remains the most important work for an understanding of Lukács's marxism.

STEDMAN JONES, G., 'The Marxism of the Early Lukács', *New Left Review*
    No. 70, 1971,
is one of the best short critical accounts. Other useful general accounts of
Lukács's thought include:
    MESZAROS, I. (*ed.*), *Aspects of History and Class Consciousness*, Routledge and
        Kegan Paul, London 1971.
    PARKINSON, G. H. R. (*ed.*) *George Lukács: the Man, his Work, and his Ideas*,
        Weidenfeld and Nicholson, London 1970.
    WATNICK, M., 'Relativism and Class Consciousness' in LABEDZ, L. (*ed.*)
        Revisionism, Allen and Unwin, London 1962.
Telos devoted two issues, Nos. 10 and 11 (1971), to Lukács and these contain a
number of interesting articles in addition to those by Federici and Kettler to
which I referred in the text.
    Lukács's pre-marxist writings on aesthetics include:
    LUKÁCS, G., *The Theory of the Novel*, Merlin Press, London 1971.
    LUKÁCS, G., *Soul and Form*, Merlin Press, London 1974.
Lukács's Rumanian follower, Lucien Goldmann, took up and used some of the
ideas present in *Soul and Form*, demonstrating again the ease with which Lukács's
pre-marxist idealism could be adapted to certain kinds of marxism:
    GOLDMANN, L., *The Hidden God*, Routledge and Kegan Paul, London 1964.
This work is in a class of its own, and is one of the most enjoyable and impressive
pieces of writing on sociology of literature to have come from this, or any other,
school of marxism.
    The best secondary source on the early Lukács is the article by Kettler in *Telos*.
    Lukács's later writings on aesthetics are collected in several volumes of essays:
    LUKÁCS, G., *Studies in European Realism*, Merlin Press, London 1975.
    LUKÁCS, G., *The Meaning of Contemporary Realism*, Merlin Press, London
        1962.
    LUKÁCS, G., *Writer and Critic*, Merlin Press, London 1970.
He has also written studies of Thomas Mann and Walter Scott, and was engaged
in writing a major theoretical work on aesthetics at the time of his death.
    For a good introduction to Lukács's aesthetics see:
    ORR, J., 'George Lukács' in ROUTH, J. and WOLFF, J. (*eds.*), *Sociology of
        Literature: Theoretical Studies*, Sociological Review Monographs, Keele 1977.
The debates between Lukács and Brecht, and between Adorno and Benjamin
are collected together in:
    BLOCH, E. *et al.*, *Aesthetics and Politics*, New Left Books, London 1978.

iv. Brecht and Benjamin
The best introduction to Brecht's writings is the collection:
    WILLETT, G. (*ed.*), *Brecht on Theatre*, Eyre Methuen, London 1973.
There is a good deal of secondary literature. One useful collection is:
    MEWS, S. and KRUST, H. (*eds.*), *Essays on Brecht*, University of North
        Carolina, Chapel Hill 1974.
These essays are uneven in quality. The most interesting are by Grimm and
Battrick. *Screen* produced a special number on Brecht—*Screen*, Vol. 15, No. 2,
London 1974.

See also:

LOVELL, A., 'A short Organum for Epic Theatre and Counter-Cinema', (unpublished).

Walter Benjamin emphasised the concept of the author as producer, and the concept of production rather than reflection was brought into prominence in recent marxist cultural studies. For an introduction to Benjamin's work, the following essays should be read:

BENJAMIN, W., 'The author as Producer' in *Understanding Brecht*, New Left Books, London 1973.

BENJAMIN, W., 'The Work of Art in the Age of Mechanical Reproduction' in *Illuminations*, Cape, London 1970.

BENJAMIN, W., 'Paris—the Capital of the Nineteenth Century' in *Charles Baudelaire*, New Left Books, London 1973.

ENZENSBERGER, H. M., 'Constituents of a Theory of the Media', *New Left Review*, No. 64, London 1970, reprinted in *Raids and Reconstructions: Essays in Politics, Crime and Culture*, Pluto Press, London 1976.

This article attempts to apply some of Benjamin's ideas to develop a theory and politics of the mass media today.

6. MARXIST AESTHETICS (2): THE CONVENTIONALIST DEVELOPMENT

For a short introduction, which is representative of the kinds of interests and concerns of marxist conventionalist aesthetics, its links with formalism, etc., see:

BENNETT, T., *Formalism and Marxism*, Methuen, London 1979.

An influential text on literature was:

MACHEREY, P., *A Theory of Literary Production*, Routledge and Kegan Paul, London 1978.

First written in 1966, it was only recently translated into English, but influenced such writers as Terry Eagleton.

i. Structuralism, Semiology and Modern Linguistics

The impact of linguistic theory on conventionalist marxism has been crucial. For an introduction, see:

GUIRAUD, P., *Semiology*, Routledge and Kegan Paul, London 1975.

CULLER, J., *Structuralist Poetics*, Routledge and Kegan Paul, London 1975.

JAMESON, F., *The Prison-House of Language*, Princeton University Press, Princeton 1972.

BARTHES, R., *Elements of Semiology*, Cape, London 1970.

There are several structuralist readers, of which the following is fairly representative and gives an idea of the range of concerns which structuralism opens up under the influence of linguistic theory:

LANE, M. (*ed.*), *Structuralism*, Cape, London 1970.

For a marxist approach to modern linguistics and poetics which is non-conventionalist see, in addition to the essay by Timpanaro mentioned above:

DELLA VOLPE, G., *Critique of Taste*, New Left Books, London 1978.

On Russian formalism, see:

ERLICH, V., *Russian Formalism*, Mouton, The Hague 1955.

ii. Applications and Developments in Film Theory

HARVEY, S., *May '68* and Film Culture, BFI, London 1980.

This is a good, sympathetic but not uncritical account of the political and intellectual background to recent developments in film theory in France and England, and provides a clear discussion of some of the central issues in debate.

For an introduction to the whole spectrum of contemporary approaches to film, there is an excellent compilation in:

NICHOLS, B. (*ed.*), *Movies and Method,* University of California Press, Berkeley 1976.

WOLLEN, P., *Signs and Meaning in the Cinema,* Secker and Warburg, London 1972.

This was influential in introducing the application of semiology to film in this country. But the main forum where this occurred was *Screen,* which, over the past decade, has introduced and developed approaches to film and cinema coming out of semiology, Althusserian marxism and Lacanian psychoanalysis.

A representative sample of its work may be found in:

Screen Reader 1: Cinema/Ideology/Politics, SEFT, London 1977.

Other journals which have contributed to the debate include: *Cultural Studies, Screen Education, The Edinburgh Magazine* and, in literature, *Red Letters.* For a different perspective, see *Jump Cut.*

For a critical analysis of *Screen:*

McDONNELL, K. and ROBINS, K., 'The Althusserian Smokescreen around Marxist Cultural Studies', in CLARKE, S. *et al., One Dimensional Marxism,* Allison and Busby, London 1980.

7. EXTRA-COGNITIVE THEORIES OF ART

On art as a form of play, the *locus classicus* is:

HUIZINGA, J., *Homo Ludens,* Temple Smith, London 1970.

A most useful introduction to romanticism is found in:

ABRAMS, M. H., *The Mirror and the Lamp,* Oxford University Press, Oxford 1953.

Psychoanalytic theory has informed earlier movements away from cognitive rationalism, most importantly, Surrealism.

BIGSBY, C. W. E., *Dada and Surrealism,* Methuen, London 1972.

This book provides a brief introduction to surrealism. See Also:

BRETON, A., *What is Surrealism?* Pluto Press, London 1978.

NADEAU, M., *History of Surrealism,* Penguin, Harmondsworth 1968.

The Frankfurt School is also interesting from this point of view. Its attempt to marry Freud and Marx leads, in aesthetic theory, to a move away from cognitive rationalism, even though they remained in the last resort committed to it.

MARCUSE, H., *One-Dimensional Man,* Sphere, London 1964.

ADORNO, T. W. and HORKHEIMER, M., *Dialectics of Enlightenment,* Allen Lane, London 1972.

The writings of the Frankfurt School are notoriously difficult to read. The Open University provides a very useful introduction:

For analysis of the work of the School, see:

JAY, M., *The Dialectical Imagination: A History of the Frankfurt School and the Institute of Social Research* 1923-50, Little, Brown and Co., Boston 1973.

SLATER, P., *The Origins and Significance of the Frankfurt School*, Routledge and Kegan Paul, London 1977.

Two important non-marxist sources of non-cognitive aesthetic theory are:
LANGER, S., *Philosophy in a New Key*, Harvard University Press, Harvard 1957.
LANGER, S., *Feeling and Form*, Routledge and Kegan Paul, London 1953.
CASSIRER, E., *Philosophy of Symbolic Form.* (3 Vols.), Yale University Press, Yale 1965.